Lost and Now Found

from the same author

Where Do I Start?
How to Navigate the Emotional Journey of Autism Parenting
Kate Laine-Toner
ISBN 978 1 83997 5 523
eISBN 978 1 83997 5 530

of related interest

Arriving Late
The Lived Experience of Women Receiving a Late Autism Diagnosis
Jodi Lamanna
ISBN 978 1 83997 5 103
eISBN 978 1 83997 5 110

Rediscovered
A Compassionate and Courageous Guide for Late Discovered Autistic Women (and Their Allies)
Catherine Asta
ISBN 978 1 80501 1 507
eISBN 978 1 80501 1 514

LOST AND NOW FOUND

A Guide to Understanding and Accepting
Yourself for Late-Discovered Autistic Adults

Kate Laine-Toner
and Suzi Payton

Foreword by Katy Elphinstone

Jessica Kingsley Publishers
London and Philadelphia

First published in Great Britain in 2025 by Jessica Kingsley Publishers
An imprint of John Murray Press

1

Copyright © Kate Laine-Toner and Suzi Payton 2025

The right of Kate Laine-Toner and Suzi Payton to be identified as the Authors of the Work has been asserted by them in accordance with the Copyright, Designs and Patents Act 1988.

Foreword © Katy Elphinstone 2025

Front cover image source: Shutterstock®.

All rights reserved. No part of this publication may be reproduced, stored in a retrieval system, or transmitted, in any form or by any means without the prior written permission of the publisher, nor be otherwise circulated in any form of binding or cover other than that in which it is published and without a similar condition being imposed on the subsequent purchaser.

A CIP catalogue record for this title is available from the British Library and the Library of Congress

ISBN 978 1 80501 101 9
eISBN 978 1 80501 102 6

Printed and bound in Great Britain by Clays Ltd

Jessica Kingsley Publishers' policy is to use papers that are natural, renewable and recyclable products and made from wood grown in sustainable forests. The logging and manufacturing processes are expected to conform to the environmental regulations of the country of origin.

Jessica Kingsley Publishers
Carmelite House
50 Victoria Embankment
London EC4Y 0DZ

www.jkp.com

John Murray Press
Part of Hodder & Stoughton Ltd
An Hachette Company

The authorized representative in the EEA is Hachette Ireland, 8 Castlecourt Centre, Dublin 15, D15 XTP3, Ireland (email: info@hbgi.ie)

For my beautiful Charlie Bravo and our perfect ND AF connection
– Kate

To my loving wife, Michaela, and our darling dog, Pepsi
– Suzi

Contents

Acknowledgements 9

Foreword by Katy Elphinstone 11

Introduction. 15

The Interviews 17

Part 1. The Journey Starts Here

    1. What Makes Us Autistic? 21

    2. Putting the Pieces Together. 27

    3. Co-occurring Conditions 37

Part 2. The Nuts and Bolts of Being Autistic

    4. Executive Functioning. 53

    5. Communication 69

    6. Sensory Processing. 81

    7. Emotions 95

    8. Masking 107

9. Anxiety and Stress 127

10. Pathological Demand Avoidance (PDA) 143

11. Rejection Sensitivity Dysphoria (RSD). 151

Part 3. Dealing with Other People

12. Disclosure 159

13. Friends. 171

14. Love and Sex 181

Part 4. The Future is Bright!

15. Passions and Interests 193

16. Getting to Know Yourself 203

17. Finding the Confidence to Be Your True Self. 215

18. Thoughts, Beliefs and the Inner Critic. 221

19. Focus on Your Strengths and Create the Life You Want 235

20. Where Do We Go from Here?. 245

Endnotes 249

Acknowledgements

Huge thanks, once again, to Lynda Cooper for giving me (and now Suzi) the opportunity to share my knowledge with the world. Thank you to the JKP editing team for refining and improving our message with such grace and kindness.

Massive thanks to our interviewees, who gave so generously with their time and their words. This book would not exist without your stories.

Thank you to Leah and Cat for your constant support. Thank you for not asking, 'How is the writing going?' when I asked you to stop.

Thanks to everyone who has supported my work all along. You really keep me going!

Thank you to Suzi for agreeing to come on this journey with me. Your words bring a sparkling presence to this book.

Kate

To my lovely mum who was likely neurodivergent herself and left the earth plane 12 years ago, far too soon, thank you for always being there, believing in me, supporting me and loving me unconditionally. Thank you for your strength, passion and kindness and your caring nature that knew no bounds. I am proud to be your daughter and I know you are with me still, shining bright through my heart, soul and spirit.

I would also like to thank my dad, Barry Payton, whose adaptability, strength and determination have been passed on to me as well as his sense of humour and love of comedy and laughter.

Thanks to my lovely sisters, June and Nicola, for their continued support, as well as my wife, Michaela, without whose support this book would not be possible.

Thank you so much Kate for asking me to co-write this book with you; I was and am honoured to be doing this.

Thank you to Jen Thomas, my coach and spiritual mentor, who has helped me do the inner work so that I can help others do theirs.

This book is also for those neurodivergent folks who:

- have always known they were different

- have received too many messages that they are too much or not enough

- have been overwhelmed by people, the environment, the school system and life in general

- didn't have their needs met for a long time and as a result are on a journey of healing

- have found themselves confused and bewildered by the unpredictability of other humans

- have hidden their true selves from the world

- are ready to unmask and celebrate their unique and wonderful selves.

Suzi

Foreword

KATY ELPHINSTONE

Dear Newly Discovered Autistic Person,

This is where your journey begins – your Yellow Brick Road.* It's important to take your bearings before setting off. To use Kate and Suzi's wise words – there's no need to rush.

The path will pass through some tricky, thorny places, but also have some wonderful views. You'll lose some things, but gain others. The destination is well worth it, since it's made up of self-knowledge and connection.

This book represents both a road map and a companion for along the way. Exactly what's needed, I think, for such a monumental journey!

(And I just wish I'd had it, for mine.)

* * *

It was empathy that led me into the world of autism.

Not my own. My son's.

---

* The concept of the Yellow Brick Road, as a quest full of challenges, comes from the children's novel *The Wonderful Wizard of Oz* by American author L. Frank Baum: https://en.wikipedia.org/wiki/Yellow_brick_road.

It was 2016. I was reading my way through a stack of *New Scientist* magazines.

I found an article on empathy. Fascinating! Finishing it, I read the rest of the magazine before starting on the next one. I got to the Letters section. There was one about the empathy article, from an autistic woman. She wrote:

> In recent years there has been recognition that many autistic people do not fail to experience empathy for other people's mental and emotional states, as was previously thought – but that we may instead be hyper-aware, and instantly overwhelmed by them, leading to immediate shutdown to protect ourselves from the excessive stimulus.[1]

In one line, this woman had rocked my world. The only reason I'd never (until this moment, that is) considered my son might be autistic was because he was so intensely, obviously, empathetic.

I didn't finish that magazine. Instead, I pulled my laptop towards me and went online. 'Do autistic people have empathy?' I typed in.

I riffled through the top results, clicking here and there. 'Disorder', 'symptoms', 'behaviour', I read. Finally, thankfully, I landed on a less alienating site: the Wrong Planet. Smiling a little, I began to explore.

In the next weeks, I spent many hours in the forums of the Wrong Planet.* One person, during a deep and interesting conversation about autistic empathy, said to me, 'You came here to learn about your son's autism. But – and forgive me if I presume – do you not think *you* might be one of us, too?'

I felt quite flattered, since I liked these people so much, but

---

* On these forums I discovered that autistic people do indeed have empathy. Indeed, we can have a quite overwhelming amount of it – not necessarily reserved just for people but often for animals, plants or trees, and even (for many of us) inanimate objects!

didn't immediately take heed. It took a nervous breakdown – which, of course, I now recognize as autistic burnout – and a psychiatrist, who used the words 'Asperger's syndrome', for it to properly sink in.

He was right, of course. I *am* autistic. As I've frequently heard said in the autistic community, it takes one to know one!

And so – unknowingly parallel to Kate and Suzi's trajectories – my roller-coaster ride of a journey began.

Now, nearly ten years have passed. I contemplate what I've been through in the meantime, and how I've come out of it more or less in one piece.

The crumbling of my reality. Everything I'd thought was true about myself, my relationships, society, the world. I'd looked a lot into trauma, before – mostly when trying to figure out what was 'wrong' with me – but this...*this* changed the landscape completely! Suddenly, everything made sense. But, at the same time, way too much about the life I'd built, without this knowledge, did not.

A lot has changed for me since then.

I can't exaggerate how difficult – but yet how important – my journey has been. I just wish I'd had Suzi and Kate's book then – to show me the way, so I would not have been so often lost. And to keep me company, so I would not so often have felt alone.

※ ※ ※

Kate and I hold weekly meetings by Zoom. We have done so for several months. I refer to her as my colleague, even though we don't technically work together. We enjoy having someone like-minded to share things with, to bounce ideas off, to lament our losses and celebrate our wins with.

I met Suzi recently, also over Zoom. We have a great deal in common. When reading their book for the first time, especially when Suzi gives examples and anecdotes, I was taken aback – 'And there I was, thinking I was unique!'

I can't think of a better duo – Kate with her eminent practicality and kindness, and Suzi with her insight and excellent coaching techniques – to guide you, newly discovered autistic person, along your own Yellow Brick Road of self-discovery.

Good luck!

Katy is the author of *How to Raise Happy Neurofabulous Children*, published by Jessica Kingsley Publishers in 2024.

Introduction

KATE

I think something we don't talk about enough is how overwhelming your life gets when you discover you are neurodivergent. It's like watching back a movie of your life but now that movie has an entirely different meaning.[1]

DAVID GRAY-HAMMOND

This is a book about what happens when you discover that you are autistic later in life, and how to move forward from that point. It is based on the experiences of autistic people in their thirties, forties, fifties and beyond, and how being autistic impacts and has impacted their lives.

It's been over a decade since I realized that I am autistic, in my early forties. At the time, I was in a solid relationship, but in myself I was confused and lost and didn't know why my life had been so difficult up to that point. Friendships had been hard. Relationships had been hard. Working in office situations had been impossible. I didn't know how to communicate my needs, or even what those needs were.

In these pages, you will read about how both Suzi and I went through years of detaching from and unravelling our previous (pre-autistic-discovery) selves. In doing this, we were able to pick out and hang on to the things that worked, and we learned to let go of the things that didn't.

We each now have what I call a 'hand-picked life'. Our home, social and work lives all revolve around and fit within our unique needs and requirements as autistic individuals. We are both far happier, far less anxious and, I feel it's fair to say, much healthier people as a result of this work.

Our goal for this book is to help you get to this point far more quickly than we did. Within these pages are our experiences and the experiences of our interviewees. All of us share deeply personal parts of our individual journeys.

We hope this will help you to feel less alone in yours.

The Interviews

KATE

When I decided to write this book, I knew that the information and advice presented could not just be from my own life; many voices had to be shared in order to present a well-rounded body of work. I asked Suzi to be my co-author as I felt her experience as a multiply neurodivergent coach, teacher/trainer and comedian would bring both a lightness and a richness to the work (and I wasn't wrong!).

I also knew that we had to hear from as many other late-discovered autistic adults as possible. It was vital that we include a wide range of ideas, experiences and advice in order for this to be the most helpful 'guidebook' possible.

We recruited our interviewees by asking for help via our respective Facebook pages and LinkedIn accounts. We ended up with 21 interviewees aged between 30 and 59, with the average age being 44. The interviewees are mostly from the UK, with one each in the US, Norway and Poland. Fifteen identify as female and six as male.

The interviews took place over April and May 2023. Transcripts were pulled for each interview and then the recordings were destroyed. We have only used first names for anonymity, and we've used pseudonyms where the information was too personal. We have edited some of the answers for clarity.

We are so incredibly grateful to all who took part. Your bravery and honesty touched us both and have made this book something truly special.

Our wonderful interviewees:

Alice	Katharine	Michelle
Bill	Klaudia	Miguel
Bridget	Kyra	Morwenna
Emma	Lauren	Nick
Hannah	Lisa	Nikki
Irene	Loren	Rico
Jeff	Lyn	Ruth

Part 1
THE JOURNEY STARTS HERE

— Chapter 1 —

What Makes Us Autistic?

KATE

> *I feel like Pinocchio, like I grew up thinking that the other children were the real children and that I wanted to be one of them. I wanted to be a real child and I wasn't. I was something different. And I think there's still an element of that, that I'm not a real person. I'm not one of the valid people.*
>
> HANNAH

I want to preface what I'm about to share by saying that I love being autistic. Learning that I am autistic changed my life in so many ways, for the better. I'll go into great detail on this in later chapters. Although at first glance it may seem that the criteria that make us autistic are all negative things, within these areas we can find the positives. Throughout this book, Suzi and I share how we've done this in our own lives.

This book deals with many aspects of what autism looks and feels like for adults. The following are the generally accepted diagnostic criteria, explained in a way we (Kate and Suzi) know to be true based on our own experiences and the experiences of our interviewees and other late-discovered autistic adults we know.

It's important to note that the way health and community services view autism is almost entirely deficit-based. This means that it's often the case that to get a formal diagnosis, we have to demonstrate that we are struggling with, suffering from or lacking in various things. I want to share these criteria with you so you understand what makes us autistic in the eyes of assessing professionals. However, these criteria are only a tiny piece of the autism pie.

Communication issues

Difficulties with communication vary from person to person. Some of us find speaking a challenge, so prefer to write, email or text. Processing delays can cause problems as well, as some of us can't quickly assimilate information and need time to understand what we've been told or what we have read. We can struggle to communicate what is happening for us in terms of emotions and sensory difficulties.

Sometimes we can feel as if we are speaking a different language to other people. The theory of double empathy is helpful here (we cover this in Chapter 5: Communication), as it explains that neurodivergent people and neurotypical people do indeed have different ways of communicating. Neither is better; they are just different. This can make it difficult to get points across and feel understood, and, likewise, understand others around us.

On a positive note, being autistic seems to create a sort of magical shorthand when we are communicating with other autistic people. Complex topics may require far less explanation when we are speaking with someone on our same neurological wavelength.

Relationship difficulties

Before learning that I am autistic, I had painful struggles with relationships and friendships. I did not have good relationship or friendship role models growing up, and so I badly winged my way through these things based on what I saw on television and in films. Also, I was masking like a champion (pretending to be someone else – see Chapter 8: Masking, for an in-depth look at this topic) so that other people would like me. This did not make for great friendships or relationships.

Often it is before we understand that we are autistic that we have the greatest difficulties in this area. Understanding our needs and what makes us tick puts us in a far better position for more successful friendships and relationships. For many of us, our best friendships and romantic partnerships will be with other neurodivergent people.

Sensory issues

Almost all autistic individuals have some sensory difficulties. Some of us are primarily sensory seekers (hypo/under-sensitive), while others are mainly sensory avoiders (hyper/over-sensitive). However, most of us are a bit of a mixture of both. For example, I love flashing lights and am very tactile, but I don't like having stuff on my hands and I require absolute silence for sleep.

Sensory difficulties can cause all sorts of problems. Hypersensitivity can make simply accessing the world difficult, as even shopping for basic groceries can be a massive assault on the senses. On the other hand, hyposensitivity can lead to boredom, which can in turn lead to anxiety and even risky behaviours.

Here again is an area where self-knowledge can lead to great joy – or at least greater comfort. Knowing that I love lights and sparkly things has led me to fill my home with these things. Understanding that my daughter's need for loud sounds causes me stress has driven me to use noise-cancelling headphones, which I find calming.

Black-and-white thinking

If we firmly believe things are one way, it can be hard for us to contemplate or come to terms with things being a different way.

This can make it difficult for us to understand that others may have contrasting views. For example, we may believe our political or religious leanings are the only correct ones. This can make it difficult for us to understand when others' viewpoints vary from ours.

It's important to keep an eye on this within ourselves. As I've got older, I've had to force myself to see the grey areas between my ideas and someone else's dissenting perspective. This has helped me in many ways. I have come to understand that my way isn't the only way and there are often many paths between A and B, and while they are different, one is not necessarily better or worse than another.

Being able to compromise in this way is useful and healthy. We have to compromise in many situations, including friendships, romantic relationships and work environments. I don't wish to be patronizing here; it's simply that I know I had to learn this in my forties and so want to share my experience with you.

Co-occurring conditions

Almost every autistic individual also has at least one other condition. I'll just mention here that other conditions like obsessive compulsive disorder (OCD), attention deficit hyperactivity disorder (ADHD) and bowel issues add layers of complexity to our lives. Chapter 3: Co-occurring Conditions covers this at length.

Difficulty understanding emotions in ourselves and others

It can take us a long time to figure out what we are feeling. For me, sometimes something will happen and I think I'm fine with it. However, a few days later I may feel that I'm hurt or angry. This can be very confusing for the other person involved in the situation. It takes time to learn about emotions and how we can best regulate them in ourselves. We talk about this in Chapter 7: Emotions.

Extreme interest in one topic

Some, but not all, of us have a passion (some call this a 'special interest'), something that we are expert in and enjoy doing or engaging in more than anything else in the world. Sometimes it can be difficult not to talk about this to others at length. Sometimes we have an intense interest in one thing for a while but then move on to something else. Some of us are keen collectors and have large collections of one type of thing or items to do with our favourite topic(s).

As discussed in Chapter 15: Passions and Interests, our hobbies and pastimes can give us enormous joy. We can find deep pleasure in pursuing our favourite topics, and rich connections with others who enjoy the same things.

Literal thinking

This can be an issue for some of us and certainly is for me. For example, I sometimes find written instructions very difficult as I read them literally. A lot of instructions (e.g. how to set up a printer) are written with the idea that the reader will be able to think beyond what is written on the page. This isn't possible for me so I find this frustrating. Sometimes if something doesn't make sense to me, I have to push myself to question whether I'm looking at it too literally.

Literal thinking can also cause issues when it comes to sarcasm and 'banter'. Sarcasm and banter can sometimes have a negative edge, even when the person speaking doesn't mean this.

Routines and structure

Many of us rely on set routines and structure to feel calm and secure. We like things to be a certain way and struggle when our routines are disrupted or when something unexpectedly changes in our environment.

We tend to need advance warning for big changes and we need to know what to expect and what is expected of us. As you settle into your newly discovered autisticness, you'll learn ways to communicate with those around you about what you need. This will help others to give you the information that you need to manage those changes.

Take your time
It took decades for you to get to this place, where you know (or strongly believe) that you are autistic. The following chapters cover all of the above and more. You can read them in whatever way works best for you - cover to cover, or dip in and out as it suits you.

However you choose to access the information Suzi and I have provided here, please take time to assimilate what you learn and work out what it means for you and your life.

— Chapter 2 —

Putting the Pieces Together

KATE

I think it's been my superpower. I don't think I could have done the stuff I've done in my life without it. It frees me up from the emotional trauma and baggage of neurotypicals.

NICK

Discovering that you are autistic will likely be one of the most cataclysmic experiences of your life. Suddenly, so many things make sense! In time, you will come to develop a much deeper understanding of yourself and what makes you tick.

We are in this late-discovered autistic place because we flew under the radar as children. We were quirky and shy. We may have been very academically able and had typical speech. Our development from baby to toddler to child to teen may have had some anomalies but was overall typical.

Many of us blundered and stumbled our way through our teens and young adulthood. We may have had relationships with varying levels of success. Many of us have struggled with friendships and jobs. And now, here we are: autistic adults trying to work out where exactly it is we fit in the world.

For most of us, our being autistic simply wasn't seen. This was due to a number of factors. Films of the 1990s like *Rain Man* and *What's Eating Gilbert Grape* gave the general public wildly skewed and painfully stereotypical versions of what autism might look like. The character in *Rain Man* is, of course, a savant – which is actually incredibly rare. On the flipside, Gilbert Grape's brother Arnie (beautifully played by Leonardo DiCaprio) has significant learning disabilities. Both characters are over-the-top, stylized representations of *some* autistic individuals. Neither did us any favours as children, teens and young adults growing up unknowingly autistic, because we didn't look like either of these tropes.

Being different in itself, for many of us, may have had negative connotations within our families. Eccentricity, transgenderism and even homosexuality may have been scorned because these were different from the norm. In fact, in some of our families (mine included), absolutely anything that was different from what society viewed as 'normal' was frowned on. Therefore, our parents (even though they also may be neurodivergent) were unlikely to acknowledge that there could have been something out of the ordinary about us. Our unusual behaviours would have been explained in ways such as 'He's just going through a phase' or 'She's such a bookworm!' or 'She's just shy' and so on.

THE MODELS OF DISABILITY

Even now, in the collective mind of the public, the idea of 'disability' is mostly about obvious physical conditions. The idea of 'hidden disabilities' has really only come into play over the past five or ten years. Certainly, the idea of autism being a disability simply wasn't a thing, even for those with severely diminished intellectual capacity. This was, and still unfortunately is, labelled as 'severe autism'. Disability was, and still often is, symbolized by a wheelchair to denote a physical disability.

The medical model

Disability has historically been viewed through the medical

model lens, which affirms that disabled people need to be treated, fixed or cured because there is something wrong with them (and this view sadly often extends to the belief that if they can't be treated, fixed or cured, they do not belong in society). Through this lens, whether or not autism was seen as a disability, our parent(s) or guardian(s) may not have been comfortable thinking that we had anything 'wrong' with us, and thus looked the other way when faced with our various, sometimes obvious, autistic traits.

The social model
A more human approach to disability is that if a person has a condition – any condition – that makes their life more difficult, then we as a society must help that person. What support can we offer to enable them to work, attend school or simply be more comfortable on a day-to-day basis? The social model takes any negativity out of the word 'disability'.

Autism 101

Autistic children grow up to be autistic adults. Therefore, autism has generally the same characteristics whatever the person's age, though the edges will grow softer over time.

There is an old medical model chestnut about a 'triad of impairments' (which you may have heard about if you have a child who has been assessed for autism). This triad asserts that a person is autistic when they have a lot of difficulties with:

- *Social communication*: The ability to express oneself in spoken words, body language, facial expressions, and so on.

- *Social interaction*: The ability to interact in a socially acceptable manner with others. This includes the ability to empathize, which many people believe autistic individuals incapable of doing (see more on this in Chapter 7: Emotions).

- *Social imagination*: The ability to put oneself in another's shoes and play out in our minds the possible repercussions of our actions.

We asked all of our interviewees how it came to be that they realized that they were autistic. The responses were varied and interesting:

- For some, once their child (or another child in the family) had been diagnosed, they realized that they had many of the same traits.

- Some had an intuition that they were autistic but weren't sure they were 'autistic enough' to merit assessment or diagnosis (or take part in this book!).

- Some stumbled on information about autism. This was especially true for our female interviewees.

- A few had a mental health breakdown or mental health issues that were incorrectly diagnosed. They knew the diagnosis wasn't correct so they began to research what else the issue might be.

- Some had a relative, friend or colleague who saw it first and suggested they may want to have an assessment.

Go with your gut

If your gut instinct is telling you that you are or might be autistic, you probably are. Most late-discovered autistic people come to see that they are autistic after a great deal of thought and research. If, after all of your own investigation and reflective thinking, you believe you are autistic, then you are.

If you haven't already got the ball rolling with getting assessed (and you feel a formal diagnosis is important), you'll want to see your doctor. They may ask you to justify why you think you are autistic. I actually had to write a letter explaining not only why I thought I was autistic but also how I felt a diagnosis would improve my life. I have heard similar experiences from others. What happens next will depend on how autism is assessed in your area. You may be referred on to an assessing team. There may be a long waiting list for an assessment.

At the time of writing, in the UK there is a scheme called Right to Choose which you may be able to access for assessment (search the internet for 'right to choose autism' to learn more). Alternatively, you may choose to pay for a private diagnosis, which will cost, on average, around £2000. There will be similar schemes in other countries.

Self-identification is perfectly OK

When I went for my assessment, I was in a very good place mental-health-wise. I was also at the time running an autism-related charity. For some reason, I went into the assessment as if it was some sort of business meeting. 'Here we are,' I thought, 'autism professionals talking about autism!' Apparently, this was not the way to go about a successful assessment. Because of my approach to the situation, I came across as positive, sociable and well spoken…and I didn't get a diagnosis.

At first, I was upset about this. I also felt like a fraud, as I didn't have a piece of paper officially saying I am autistic. However, I soon learned that self-identification is perfectly valid. That is what I chose to do, and since then I've not felt the need to pursue an 'official' diagnosis.

Waiting for an assessment and getting a diagnosis are not easy or straightforward situations. If you are unable to achieve these things, and your research and gut feelings tell you that you are autistic, then self-identification is fine. This is why we refer in this book to 'late-discovered' autistic adults as opposed to 'late-diagnosed', as not all of us will get a diagnosis.

Everyone is different, however, and if you feel the need to have a formal assessment and diagnosis, by all means pursue this. Some people in the UK find that they are unable to get a diagnosis through the National Health Service (NHS) but go on to have success with a private assessor.

> **ARE YOU DISABLED?**
>
> Whether or not you choose to identify as disabled is up to you. The Equality Act 2010[1] defines disability as a physical or mental impairment that has a long-term impact on a person's ability to carry out day-to-day activities. If this definition resonates with you, you may want to think about whether or not to refer to yourself as disabled.
>
> Earlier in this chapter, I mention the medical and social models of disability, two very different viewpoints. There is no shame in being, identifying or claiming that you are disabled. If you believe that you are disabled, there are likely financial and other benefits you may be entitled to. Have a look at your government's website to find out what is available to you.[2]

Big feelings

However it is that you come to understand that you are, or likely are, autistic, you will probably experience a range of emotions:

- Happy that you finally understand why you are the way you

are, and why life has been such a challenge for you. One of our interviewees, Lauren, said, 'For me, it's kind of like a lot of things make sense, and my struggles are explained.'

- Sadness that you had to wait so long. There may also be sadness that life might have been so different if you had been diagnosed at a younger age. You may also feel sad that when you did not understand that you are autistic, you may have said or done things that caused other people distress.

- Embarrassment over some of the things you've done, now that you are looking at them through an autistic lens.

- Relief at finally understanding that there is nothing wrong with you; you are just autistic. Jeff told me that realizing that he is autistic was 'like a eureka moment'. He shared that although he has had some success, like going to school, graduating with advanced degrees and managing to have a career, he:

    > felt like a failed human. I had very little self-esteem and lots of shame. I didn't know how things were supposed to work. But [once I realized I am autistic] I had the answer. I wasn't a broken human being, which is what I felt like with my different memory issues and all of these things. I'm a perfectly normal autistic person, and there are reasons for everything.

- Anger that your parents didn't see it or wouldn't acknowledge it. For some, this anger is to do with the fact that their caregivers did see it and actually had them assessed and diagnosed, but never told them; they had to figure it out on their own. Once they had a diagnosis and mentioned it to their parent(s), they found out the truth (in their thirties or forties or later, after struggling with so many things in life).

- Freedom to be yourself and embrace your autisticness. Nick explained:

  > I almost don't want to fit in anymore. I'm almost deliberately trying not to. Rock the boat and see what happens. I think there's an element of us autistics that we like to throw a little grenade in and see what happens.

- Confusion about why your autisticness wasn't spotted earlier as it's so obvious to you when you look back on your childhood, teen years and young adulthood.

- Anxiety and apprehension about explaining being autistic to your friends and family, particularly if you are self-identifying. I definitely have this as I sometimes worry it may come across that I am using being autistic as an excuse for 'bad' behaviour – for example, poor communication that has caused upset.

- Overwhelm about what you need to do next and where to start with moving forward from here.

- Feelings of being a fraud. This is very common – some of us worry we are not 'autistic enough' to merit diagnosis. Bridget explained how it took her a very long time to see that she is autistic. After her son was diagnosed as autistic, she began looking for the hereditary link. She could see it in her husband but not in herself. She said, 'I was like, "Am I? Am I not? I don't know...and if I am, then this changes everything. And if I'm not, then what?"' She subsequently was assessed and diagnosed as autistic:

  > I still do get wobbly about it, where I think, 'Oh, God, maybe I'm not. Maybe it's a mistake. Maybe they didn't

assess me properly. Maybe it's all a lie and it's all gonna come crashing down.' But the more I think about it I realize it's not a lie.

Miguel has experienced feeling like a fraud as well. He shared with me that there have been times when he has disclosed being autistic and the response has been along the lines of 'Really? But you are so capable; you do so much!' as if to say that being autistic and being able are mutually exclusive.

So, what do you do now?
There's a lot to get your head around here, and it can be difficult to work out what is most important. Tell your partner/friends/family/employer? Completely change everything in your life that isn't working? Please don't rush into anything. First, you need stability.

Learning that you are autistic will rock your world (not always in a good way). It may even feel as if a bomb's gone off in your life. You will begin to question your life choices. It may suddenly become glaringly obvious that some huge things need to change and this can be scary.

Quiet baby steps
Once you understand that you are autistic, the best thing to do is feed yourself information. This and other books written by autistic adults will be incredibly helpful and comforting as you find your way through a world that will feel very new to you.

Begin to let your autistic self out to play. Embrace your quirks and your stims (stims are self-stimulatory behaviours that we use to calm ourselves; more on this in Chapter 6: Sensory Processing). Wear the clothes that feel comfortable to you. Eat the food that feels safe to you.

Be kind to yourself

First and foremost, I need you to know that you are going to be OK. You will get through this.

On average, it took our interviewees around two years to get their heads round the idea that they are autistic. Of course, self-discovery is a lifelong process, but the bulk of the work was done in the first few years.

I was mortified when I learned that I am autistic and looked back on some of the things I'd done and said. It's difficult to not beat ourselves up for the sins of our past. I like to remember the Maya Angelou quote, 'Do the best you can until you know better. Then, when you know better, do better.' And so it is for us newly discovered autistics.

You did not know, when you were 12 or 18 or 25, that you were autistic. You may feel you have done many cringeworthy things and said many tactless things. So what? Everyone says or does embarrassing things at some point in their lives. Those things are in the past. Please forgive yourself and move on.

You are not alone

It's common for autistic people to feel alone and as if we are the only ones going through what we are going through. However, what we found through our interviews, by consuming the content of autistic authors and bloggers and our own experiences, is that this simply isn't true.

We're all in this together.

— Chapter 3 —

Co-occurring Conditions

SUZI

Autism rarely travels alone and it's likely that you will experience other conditions alongside being autistic. Often people are surprised – and sometimes relieved – to learn that some challenges (and strengths) are a result of one or a combination of the following:

- ADHD
- Tourette's syndrome
- anxiety
- depression
- OCD
- sensory processing differences
- auditory processing disorder
- dyslexia
- dyspraxia
- dyscalculia
- giftedness (2e)
- aphasia
- bowel conditions
- eating disorders/disordered eating
- prosopagnosia (face blindness).

This chapter serves as a brief overview of co-occurring conditions.

Due to the complexity and number of them, they each could have a book of their own! Co-occurring conditions are complex. I am autistic, have ADHD, OCD and Tourette's, and I still find myself puzzling over what is what!

Attention deficit hyperactivity disorder (ADHD)

Attention deficit hyperactivity disorder (ADHD) is (narrowly in my opinion) characterized by difficulties with concentration, attention, hyperactivity and impulsivity. As an autistic ADHDer myself, I can honestly say that there is so much more to ADHD than what the title suggests.

Unfortunately, there are still some outdated stereotypes regarding ADHD – the main one being that only little boys can have it, and that it is mainly about hyperactivity. This simply is not true.

There are four types of ADHD:

- *Inattentive ADHD:* The person with this type of ADHD is likely to miss details when doing such things as completing forms and reading text. They may zone out/daydream during conversations or during meetings. This person may also regularly lose things such as keys – and passports! I once put my passport in a 'safe' place only to completely forget where that was. I searched high and low and was about to order a new one when I found it among a pile of clothes in the bottom of my wardrobe!

- *Hyperactive ADHD:* Hyperactivity can be visible – for example, fidgeting, moving frequently, having to always do something with the hands and needing to be always 'doing' something. It can also be hidden, such as having racing thoughts and a brain that never stops. It can show through high-energy talking, with few or rare pauses for breath, as well as unintentionally interrupting when others are speaking. This is something that can create shame within individuals, so it is really important to recognize that your intentions are not to hurt others and it's not your fault.

- *Impulsive ADHD:* Impulsivity can show up through impulse buying, finishing others' sentences, making quick decisions without thinking them through and being quick to react if feeling threatened or insulted. The person with this type of ADHD may often (several times a day) have a thought and feel compelled to follow it through, such as, 'I wonder when dinosaurs became extinct?' and stop whatever they are doing to look it up.

- *Combined ADHD:* This person is both impulsive and hyperactive. This can be very tiring!

A key component of ADHD is being easily and often constantly distracted – for example, starting one task then moving on to another before finishing the first one, sometimes without realizing it happened. Memory is another challenge – in particular, working memory, where the ability to hold information in mind while thinking of something else causes many issues throughout life. My working memory is so poor that if I try to transfer information from a Word document to a spreadsheet, I often forget what the data is in the short time switching between programs, which is very frustrating!

Also, concentration can be difficult, especially if there is no interest involved, and is extremely tiring. When transferring quotes for this book on to a spreadsheet, I had a meltdown later that day from the extended concentration required, as well as a headache from looking intently at the screen and words.

I could literally write all day about ADHD and autism; they are my passions after all. I believe that ADHD and autism are such a contradiction that they cover each other up and make it difficult to identify which is which. Many AuDHDers (autistic and ADHD folk) talk of their autistic side craving routine and their ADHD side hating routine! It definitely is a fine balancing act to get the two parts working together, and when you do, the sense of flow and accomplishment is a fine thing!

Tourette's syndrome

Tourette's syndrome is a tic disorder, and tics can be anywhere from mild to extreme and involve involuntary sounds or movements. For a diagnosis of Tourette's, tics must be present for at least 12 months.

Tics are involuntary sounds and movements. Often people mistake these for 'nervous twitches' or 'habits'. They are neither of these things; they are tics. I know of people who visited their doctor for a sniffing tic and were misdiagnosed as having allergies.

There are different types of tics. Simple motor tics can range from excessive eye blinking, shoulder shrugging, nose twitching, jaw stretching and muscle clenching, to name a few. These are known as simple motor tics.

There are also simple vocal tics. These include throat clearing, whistling, sniffing, grunting and even animal sounds.

Other types of tics include complex motor tics, such as jumping, twirling, touching yourself, objects or others, making obscene gestures and copying other people's gestures.

There are also complex vocal tics such as repeating the words and phrases of others, which is known as echolalia. Another complex vocal tic is to do with saying words or phrases out of context. I have had these kinds of tics, and I've spent many a moment wondering why I have just said such random things. Because I was so socially anxious and had a massive fear of judgement and ridicule, I covered these tics up by laughing and pretending I'd said what I said on purpose. This was all before I knew what tics were, and it shows the depths us neurodivergent folk go to cover up and mask our true, unique and wonderful selves, doesn't it?

Other complex vocal tics include saying socially unacceptable words and phrases. There is a myth that Tourette's syndrome is only to do with swearing tics, but only 10 per cent of people with Tourette's have these.

My tics are very mild these days and pretty much go by unnoticed, especially to the uninitiated. However, in the past they were very prominent, obvious, painful and tiring.

It is worth mentioning that pretty much every human being will experience tics in their lifetime, and one or two tics do not constitute a diagnosis. However, as tics are not well understood, it is worth looking into if this is something you feel you experience. Having tics can be exhausting, especially if, like me, you spend a lot of precious energy holding them in (some can be suppressed, but at a cost).

Tics can also cause feelings of embarrassment and shame. Just knowing what is going on can be enough to relieve some of the tension and anxiety that goes along with having them. Also, if you know what you are dealing with, you can ask for accommodations such as switching the camera off in virtual meetings, taking extra breaks to 'release' tics in private and so on.

Depression

Due to the wide range of challenges autistic adults face, we are prone to experiencing periods of depression. Depression is a common and sometimes serious mental health condition. If you are depressed, you will experience chronic feelings of sadness and hopelessness. You may also find it difficult to take part in activities you would normally enjoy.

Some other symptoms of depression include changes in sleep and eating and extreme tiredness. You may struggle to focus on things. Feelings of guilt and worthlessness are also common with depression.

If you are feeling any of these things, please seek help. See your doctor to find out what options are available to you. Talking therapies can help, especially if the therapist or counsellor has experience of autism and other neurodivergent conditions. Antidepressant medication may help as well.

Obsessive compulsive disorder (OCD)

Obsessive compulsive disorder (OCD) is a mental health condition that manifests as obsessions such as intrusive thoughts or fears, and compulsions that serve to cancel out the obsessions.

It is important to distinguish between autistic 'behaviour' and OCD as the two can be misunderstood and mistaken for each other. For example, when we think about stimming, this is generally done for enjoyment and/or to soothe, so if an autistic person is stimming by repeatedly switching a light on and off, they may be enjoying the sounds, sensations and the visual stimulus. If this behaviour is being driven by OCD, then it may be serving as a compulsion which is distressing and serves to cancel out the obsession – for example, 'If I turn this light on and off 20 times, then my family won't die.'

As with all matters of neurodivergence, there are many myths that continue to be reinforced. OCD has its own myths, one of them being that it is all about washing hands and checking locks, and it is often associated with extreme tidiness, which is a huge contradiction when you consider that hoarding is also an element of OCD.

For me personally, my OCD is what is known as 'pure OCD'. This means that I experience distressing intrusive thoughts, and instead of carrying out physical rituals such as checking doors are locked, hand washing and so on, I try to extinguish the intrusive thought with a different more pleasant one.

Often the press and media leave out the intrusive thoughts side of OCD and focus on the 'behaviours' that can be seen. This and a lack of awareness contribute to the myths and stereotypes around this highly distressing condition.

OCD is treatable and not something you have to accept is part of you. If you feel you may have OCD, then please do check out the OCD Action website and speak to your GP or primary care physician to get help. It is a horrible condition to be dealing with, and once you understand that the obsessions are not real, you can start to manage it. One phrase that helps me when I have a flare-up is repeating to myself, 'It's not me, it's OCD', while practising deep-breathing techniques.

Auditory processing disorder (delayed processing)

Many autistic folks report that they have a lag or delay when processing what they hear. This can happen occasionally or frequently and can even be affected by quality of sleep and how stressed/overwhelmed/overstimulated a person is. It can be worse when there is background noise.

Often people talk of asking a person to repeat what they have just said, only to catch up and 'hear' before they have completely repeated it, which can cause confusion and misunderstandings. I personally experience this a lot and get frustrated if the person repeats what they have said in a louder and slower way. Did I say 'frustrated'? I meant to say that instant fury is unleashed!

Central auditory processing disorder (CAPD)

Central auditory processing disorder (CAPD) is a complex disorder. Teri James Bellis explains:

> The hearing itself is fine, but what gets into the ear somehow gets jumbled by the time it gets to the brain. Because of this, different letters may sound the same to you, making it hard to tell the difference between different speech sounds. Or you might hear what someone is saying, but it's distorted or muffled, like the person is mumbling, especially if there is lots of noise around.[1]

There is no cure for CAPD, but there are supports and strategies that you can put in place to help:

- Sit near a wall/in a corner of a room where some of the environmental sounds can be absorbed by the wall.

- Sit at the front in training/education settings to have a better chance of hearing the facilitator/teacher.

- Use subtitles when watching TV/video.

- Ask for instructions to be written down/emailed.

- Adapt your environment where possible – for example, ask for the printer/photocopier to be moved away from you.

- Ask people to move to a quieter space for conversations if there is background noise.

- Take regular breaks – people with CAPD work harder to concentrate and pay attention than those without it.

Dyslexia

Dyslexia is a learning difficulty that impacts a person's ability to read and write. It is actually an information processing disability. Individuals with dyslexia may have issues with processing and recalling information that they see, read or hear. Dyslexia causes problems with learning and literacy skills. It can also affect a person's organizational skills.

Many neurodivergent people are diagnosed with dyslexia, often in their school years, before any other condition, and, as we know, it is only part of the picture.

Dyspraxia/developmental coordination disorder (DCD)

Dyspraxia, also known as developmental coordination disorder (DCD), affects balance, coordination and movement.

Dyspraxic people may experience (to varying degrees) difficulties with fine and gross motor skills such as handwriting or throwing and catching a ball. Coordination can be affected, as well as organization skills and speech and language.

It is clear to see how many of these co-occurring conditions have similar presentations, which is why neurodivergence is so complex and tricky to identify and distinguish. Sometimes I just accept that I won't always know what part of me is causing which issue.

Dyscalculia

Dyscalculia is a learning disability which causes difficulty in working with numbers. This creates issues with mathematics, but also can cause problems with understanding time and working with money.

If, like me, you experience 'maths anxiety', you will know that the trauma is real. The difficulties associated with having a poor concept of numbers has caused me a lifetime of shame and frustration, not to mention getting into £20,000 worth of debt! The debt is now paid off and the ADHD under control, so my number difficulties are easier to manage now. I now ask for help with any decisions to do with money, as well as basic maths problems. My self-esteem and self-worth are no longer tied to how good or bad I am at maths, and I proudly count on my fingers when I need to and am ready to advocate for myself if anyone comments!

Giftedness/2e

Growing up, I developed a conflicting sense of self where I knew I was skilled in some areas and very unskilled in others. I would often wonder how I could be so good at sports and writing stories yet so terrible at maths and science. The difference in abilities is often referred to as a 'spiky profile', which most neurodivergent people have.

This conflict within me resulted in low self-esteem, low confidence and extreme self-doubt. I took cues from the people around me as to who I should be, how I should act and even what type of words to use. I distinctly remember using a 'big' factual word in general conversation and being laughed at. This led me to develop a huge fear of being laughed at for appearing 'stupid', so unconsciously I started to play small, keep my opinions to myself and do everything I could to avoid being laughed at (unless I was being funny on purpose, which I became very good at). (The irony here is not lost on me as I write this 30 or so years later that the big, factual word I used made me far from stupid.)

Being gifted is something that society in general has an issue with talking about as it is seen as somehow 'big-headed' and arrogant to admit to, never mind discuss.

A term that is used when autistic/neurodivergent folks are gifted/highly able in some areas is called '2e', which means twice exceptional.

Giftedness can relate to 'superior vocabulary, advanced ideas and opinions, high levels of creativity and problem-solving ability, extreme curiosity, wide range of interests not related to school, penetrating insight into complex issues, specific talent or consuming interest area, and a sophisticated sense of humour'.[2]

There are many reasons why autistic people are not identified/diagnosed until later in life, and one factor that can play a part is if they are gifted in some way. Many adults are not identified as kids because they are twice-exceptional (2e) and their gifts help overshadow the challenges. This has certainly been my experience, and it has taken a long time to come to terms with, but I am getting there. This is why knowledge, understanding and self-awareness are critical if we are to truly understand ourselves and so that others can understand us, too.

Aphantasia

Aphantasia is a condition characterized by an inability to voluntarily create mental images in one's mind.

Key characteristics:

- Inability to 'picture' things in the mind's eye.
- Difficulty with visual memory.
- Challenges with imagination-based tasks.
- Normal ability to recognize faces and objects, but inability to visualize them when not present.

Jeff's aphantasia experience

Have you heard of aphantasia? Try picturing an apple in your mind. Most people can do this but I can't, I just see blackness. I also don't have visual dreams. I don't see people, objects or anything in my mind at all. I also don't recall past events well. It is a condition called severely deficient autobiographical memory, or SDAM for short. There is research being done to see if aphantasia and SDAM might be related.

When I see a photograph of myself from a past event, I normally won't recall anything about it. The past events that I do remember will often have something unusual about them. They might have been fun, or something really funny happened, or perhaps something that was traumatic. I might remember a few specific details and facts about it, but that is all. For a long time, I hid this part about myself, and wouldn't talk to anyone about it. It can lead to stressful situations. I have dealt with a lot of shame about it.

I'll give you an example. I can recognize faces just fine. Let's pretend I see someone walking towards me whom I should know and have met many times. I will likely recognize them, but I won't recall from where. I won't remember their name or much of anything else. I might recall in what area of my life I know them, like a teacher at my son's school. This type of thing has happened to me with people I have known for a really long time, and consider friends. I have to sort of fake my way through the conversation, pretending I recall stuff that we've done or talked about, even though I can't recall a thing. I have been fortunate to have met other autistic people like me who have both aphantasia and SDAM.

Bowel issues

There appears to be a higher prevalence of bowel issues – such as constipation, irritable bowel syndrome (IBS), diarrhoea and diverticulitis. There is no clear reason for this, but it may be useful to know if you suffer from a bowel condition.[3]

Eating disorders/disordered eating

Autistic individuals are more likely than their non-autistic counterparts to have an eating disorder such as avoidant restrictive food intake disorder (ARFID), anorexia nervosa or bulimia. There is also a higher prevalence of disordered eating among autistic adults. Disordered eating refers to restrictive eating practices – for example, following very strict diets to extreme levels (ketogenic, raw food, gluten-free, strict veganism, etc.).[4]

> ### Kate's disordered eating journey
> I have always had an interest in food and nutrition. When I was in my thirties, I began to experiment with alternative ways of eating, such as following a raw food diet or gluten-/dairy-free diet (not due to any intolerance). I would dabble in one way of eating for a while, then go back to eating in whatever way was 'normal' for me at the time.

Over time, these eating regimes would become more and more restrictive. At the start of the pandemic, I began to follow a ketogenic vegan diet. This is very extreme and requires a lot of specialist ingredients that were not always easy to source at that time. I followed this for a few months. It's important to note that this was a stressful time due to lockdowns and general pandemic issues, and that just before Covid hit, I split up with my partner.

A few years ago, I finally realized that these diets are very unhealthy for me. If I was following a specific plan, and I went somewhere that didn't have any food that fitted into that plan, I wouldn't eat. I would spend a lot of money on specific ingredients and supplements. I would lose weight very quickly and then rapidly gain it back when I went back to eating normal food.

What was this about? Control. When I look back on the times when I was most feverishly following a certain plan, these were times when I felt most out of control. Food is one area we all have complete control over. I loved the control of eating only very specific things. It's fair to say I also loved the interoceptive hit of often feeling extremely hungry.

I'm happy to say I've now broken the habit of disordered eating. I am still tempted by extreme diets, but I work at keeping myself on track. I now prefer to eat intuitively – I eat whatever I want but only when I'm hungry. It's a work in progress, but I'm glad to be out of the disordered eating cycle.

Prosopagnosia (face blindness)

Some autistic individuals struggle with prosopagnosia, which can manifest in a number of different ways. It may be the case that they cannot recognize faces at all, or it may be that they struggle to differentiate between faces of strangers or people they do not know well. Some find that they can only recognize known people in a specific environment, such as at work or in the person's home. People with prosopagnosia rely on clues such as voice, clothing and hair style/colour to be able to identify people and can find it difficult if these things change. They may also study people's movements and mannerisms as a way to differentiate between people.

— Part 2 —

THE NUTS AND BOLTS OF BEING AUTISTIC

— Chapter 4 —

Executive Functioning

KATE

> With things like time blindness, it's about, 'OK, I don't have a concept of time, so what can I put in place, rather than [think that] I need to get a concept of time?' Because then you're trying to be someone you're not. It's letting that go, isn't it?
>
> MORWENNA

Executive functioning is essentially about our ability to organize ourselves to carry out the various tasks we need to do to get through life. Almost all neurodivergent people struggle with executive functioning. Exccutive functioning difficulties are what make us late and disorganized, and can make us feel like a failure (when we are not).

Executive functioning problems are at the core of why some of us think things like 'Why can't I get anything done? Why is life so hard?' Until and unless we can truly get our head round how to support ourselves with executive functioning, life can be a struggle.

Executive functioning encompasses three main things:

- Memory:
  - Finding/acquiring/organizing all of the information, tools and supplies needed to carry out the task.

- Remembering how it went the last time you carried out this task and if there is any new information you need.
- Debriefing – thinking about how you could do things differently this time or next time to make life easier.

- Cognitive flexibility:
  - Prioritizing where to start the task and the steps involved in carrying out the task.
  - Recovering when you are interrupted or distracted, or if the guidelines around the task are confusing or disrupted.

- Impulse control:
  - Starting and staying with the task until completion; not getting sidetracked by other things or by an emotional response you have while completing the task.
  - Overcoming perfectionism about how certain aspects of the task should be.

Poor executive functioning is at the heart of scenarios like 'I need to do my taxes and the deadline is today but first I'm going to put my books in order of rainbow colours' and 'I need money to get a train ticket to visit my family but I bought equipment for a new hobby instead'.

LET'S BREAK IT DOWN

The easiest way to explain how executive functioning works is to give an example from my life. My biggest executive functioning bugbear is posting greeting cards. There is just something about posting cards that I find super hard. (There are literally three – three! – sympathy cards sitting in my kitchen right now, waiting to be posted. I'm taking bets on whether or not this will happen...) I'll break down the points above and apply them to this scenario so you can see what they look like in the day-to-day.

Finding/acquiring/organizing all of the information, tools and/or supplies needed to carry out the task

'I need to buy a card. I've already got a first-class stamp, a pen and the person's address. I'll also need a postbox – I'll use that one in the village that collects at 4.45pm.'

Prioritizing where to start the task and the steps involved in carrying out the task

'I know from having done this loads of times that I need to get the card, write in it, seal the envelope, write the address on the envelope, stick the stamp on and put the card in the postbox. Simple, right?'

Remembering how it went the last time you carried out this task and if there's any new information you need

'Last time I didn't post the card in time. I am probably not going to post the card in time this time either. Oh well. Ah – I remember now that stamps have changed to a new format since I last posted a card so I'll need to get some new stamps.'

Staying with the task until completion and not getting sidetracked by other things or by an emotional response you have while completing the task

(Note that if there is an emotional response, being sidetracked is guaranteed.)

'I am just going to write in this card... I don't know what to say. I haven't seen her for such a long time and we had that funny thing the last time we spoke... Hmm, I really should re-pot that plant on the windowsill. Do I have any compost? I think I need special compost for succulents. I'll just look on Amazon. Oh, I'll need a new pot as well...'

Recovering when you are interrupted or distracted, or if the guidelines around the task are confusing or disrupted
'No! I just need to take two minutes and write in this card!' Also: 'Hang on, didn't she move to another part of the city? I'll text our mutual friend to get her current address.' And later: 'Oh shit! That late collection postbox is now a 9am collection one! I'll need to find a different postbox, or resign myself to the fact that now the card will definitely be late.'

Overcoming perfectionism about how certain aspects of the task should be
'My handwriting is so messy. Will she even be able to read this? And I had to scratch that word out to correct myself because I wasn't paying attention to what I was writing. I should find another card. No, no, this will have to do. I'm just going to seal the envelope and be done with it. It is the thought that counts after all, right?'

Debriefing – thinking about how we could do things differently next time to make life easier
'This was more stressful than it should have been. I'm going to put my friends' birthdays in my phone with reminders ten and seven days before the day so I remember to send a card on time. I'll also stock up on stamps and buy a bunch of cards so I have some on hand.' (All great ideas but it's a whole new executive functioning job to then carry out these plans.)

Life involves a vast number of decisions

You can see from this breakdown that although sending a card seems a simple task at first glance, it involves a LOT of decisions, thought processes and micro-tasks within the main task. It's important to note that our lives are full of such simple-but-complicated chores. Even if you think about making a cup of tea, there are so many steps (and yes, I know these may not be *your* tea brewing steps but I'm just making a point here):

- Fill the kettle.
- Turn on the kettle.
- Get out a cup.
- Choose a tea.
- Find the tea.
- Put a teabag in the cup.
- Put sugar in the cup.
- Pour water into the cup.
- Stir the tea.
- Remove the teabag.
- Get out the milk – is the milk OK?
- Put the milk in.
- Stir the tea.

Fourteen steps! The same can be true of getting dressed, preparing a sandwich, paying bills and so on. The point I am making is that for those of us with differently wired brains, what seem like 'simple things' for neurotypical people are anything but for us.

Why these things are hard for us

All day long, every person's brain is filtering vast amounts of information, determining which bits are important and which bits to let go of. This includes all of the sensory stimuli as well. Autistic individuals have a far more difficult time doing this, which can cause us to become mildly to very overwhelmed. Instead of putting our attention on something crucial (I must pay these overdue bills), we can get distracted and hyperfocus on something that isn't essential (I'm going to spend two hours reorganizing my wardrobe). This is because the distracting thing is often more calming and/or stimulating than the important task at hand.

The essential thing I want you to get here is that this is OK. You are not flawed. There is nothing wrong with you, and you are not a failure. You just have a different brain, and over time, you will find ways of working with your brain instead of against it. Life will get much easier when you do this.

Shame and more shame

When we struggle with executive functioning, it can cause a lot of shame. We must break out of 'Why can't I do this? It should be easy!' sort of thinking. This is an area where we really must develop self-compassion and understanding of our own differences. It doesn't matter if you struggle with something that other people find easy. That's just part of you, and it's OK.

One of our interviewees shared her issues with laundry. Like many life tasks, washing clothes has a lot of steps, and the fact that there are big time gaps in the steps creates issues. For this person, sometimes it is difficult to remember to take the washing out of the machine and hang it to dry. So, a day or so may pass, and she'll realize the washing is still in the machine and now needs to be re-washed as it's starting to smell. For this woman, laundry feels like a basic thing that she should be able to manage, but because of how her brain works, it can be difficult.

We can really struggle with the fact that in our lives we can manage all sorts of huge things, but a task we deem to be 'simple' completely levels us. Sarah said:

I've done all of these incredible projects all over the world. I'm very intelligent, but the admin side of things is really difficult for me. I find writing invoices and sending invoices hard in a way that doesn't even make any sense to me.

Adding to the shame is the issue of other people witnessing and criticizing our executive functioning struggles. Morwenna shared:

> There's a mental health aspect to it there as well. And then if somebody else is around, I might feel ashamed in front of them. So, there's kind of layers of it. And some days I can do it and I can remember, and other days I can't or I don't.

It is likely that for most of your life, other people have commented negatively about your inability to carry out certain tasks. As late-discovered autistics, we all grew up with parents or carers who had no idea about our neurodivergence and who may have been very impatient with our inability to tidy our rooms, get homework done on time and so on. Growing up, you may have had unhelpful comments from parents, teachers, coaches and other adults in your life. As an adult, you may have friends and partners who are equally baffled, frustrated and annoyed by your challenges.

All of these negative messages come together to form one huge stick we beat ourselves with, often viciously.

Be kind and gentle with yourself

If you are finding life difficult and you can't work out why it's impossible to get anything done, please cut yourself some slack. Tasks that are easy for your neurotypical friends, co-workers and family members may be hard for you. The same goes for tasks that appear easy for your neurodivergent friends, co-workers and family members, but aren't for you. We are all very different, with different co-occurring conditions, energy levels, lifestyles and so on.

If you are struggling, don't beat yourself up for it. Just do what you need to do to help yourself. At first it may feel awkward to provide yourself with 'reasonable accommodations' for your life. We can get overly hung up on thoughts like 'I am an adult; I should be able to manage this'. Please understand that being an adult has nothing to do with your ability to manage putting away your clean washing, or whatever other 'easy' task you find most difficult.

We can put in place some useful workarounds to help us in our day-to-day lives. Please bear in mind that the following are just some ideas that may help you manage. Some will work for you and some won't. Some will be useful ideas to store away for some future time.

Use lists, visuals and alarms

If you have something in your life that is a consistent struggle for you, you may want to try writing out the steps required to carry out that task. You could just put this in the notes app in your phone, or physically write or type and print out the steps. (I go one further and laminate the list.) Put the list where it will help you most – stuck on a door or the fridge, or with the supplies needed to do that particular task.

Please be aware that sometimes your mental health may require you to do this even for basic, daily tasks such as brushing your teeth and showering. Having visible lists for these kinds of activities can also be a prompt to do them when you might otherwise struggle to remember to bathe and brush your teeth. It's OK if you need this level of reminding. If you are struggling, this will be excellent self-care as you are reminding yourself to look after your physical self.

You can use visuals as well. Many autistic individuals are highly visually orientated and visual learners. Making visual sequences for whatever you struggle with will help you get things done, especially if you are learning something new. Visuals are not just for children! We can all benefit from visual cues sometimes.

Visuals and lists can also be useful for things that happen infrequently. I've got notes in my phone about how to put up the Christmas tree and what I must remember to pack when going on holiday. Each time I use these notes I amend them as needed as well, adding new information or deleting a redundant point.

Alarms can be a godsend. Alarms to tell us when the pasta or food in the oven needs checking, or an alarm to remind us to hang up the wet washing before it goes mouldy and needs rewashing – these are very helpful. I have a Google Nest device in my home that I program with all sorts of alarms and reminders. It's so useful!

Everything in its right place

I am autistic and also have ADHD. As I've got older, I've had to learn how to be organized. This has been no small feat! My life is quite stressful, so my home must be as neat and orderly as possible. For me, this means that everything must have a place, and must return to that place when I'm done with it.

Basic tools live under the sink in the kitchen and less-used tools live in the airing cupboard. Craft things go in the craft box. Grains, seeds and nuts have a dedicated place. I even have a dedicated drawer for 'adhesives' – glue, tape, Blu Tack and so on. I take things out and I put them away. This has made my life much simpler and has indeed reduced stress as I always know where to find things.

You might even find it useful to label cupboards, drawers and containers to make getting and staying organized easier. If you want to pursue this idea, please take a slow and steady approach. Reorganize and label just one or two things. For example, start with organizing just your tools or just your underwear drawer. Don't set out to sort out your entire home all at once as you will become overwhelmed, and this may cause you to be mean to yourself if you can't get it all done.

Pay for help

If you can afford to pay for help, do this. A cleaner can make a world of difference. Dropping your laundry off for someone else to do might be life-changing. If this is beyond your means (it is beyond mine, so I understand), perhaps you could swap something you find easy with something a friend finds easy. For example, if you enjoy cooking, perhaps you could batch-cook some meals for a friend who can give you a few hours of cleaning. Or maybe you have a friend who can help you. I enjoy cooking for a friend who simply pays me for ingredients. This gives both of us joy, so it's a win-win situation.

Break bad habits and routines

We are autistic. As such, we can sometimes find ourselves stuck in rigid routines that don't serve us well. A great example of this for me is how I use my dishwasher.

I have lived in my flat for around six years now, and I have always had a dishwasher. Until very recently, I rarely used my dishwasher as I had a rigid set of thoughts around only wanting to fill it when I had enough dirty stuff to do that. I cook a lot, and my daughter and I generate a huge amount of washing up. Instead of putting things in the dishwasher, I was hand-washing dishes six to eight times a day.

About a month ago, I made a conscious decision to change this pattern. I started emptying the dishwasher while I was waiting for the kettle to boil and the milk to warm for my morning coffee (this takes around three minutes). Then I put dishes in the dishwasher as I use them throughout the day. I turn the dishwasher on when we go to bed and repeat the process the next day.

To many people, this would seem like a totally obvious scenario. It took me SIX YEARS to figure out that doing it this way would change my life. My kitchen is always tidy now. I no longer run out of cutlery because it's all at the bottom of the sink, waiting to be washed.

The point I'm making is that we can change. If something isn't working, we can fix it. We are grown-ups and we can find work-arounds. As Morwenna said:

> Not every hack is going to work for everyone, but try them on for size and find one that works. And if you need to, you might have to change it up, especially if you have ADHD as well. You've got to be flexible all the time.

If there is a particular thing in your life that you find difficult, you have the power to change that to make your life easier. For a while, I subscribed to an e-card service that I could use to send birthday cards on the day, and this was helpful for me. As I mentioned above, you might find that paying for a laundry service or a cleaner saves a lot of drama.

It can be hard to shift our minds into new routines. Even positive change can be difficult but it can be worth it for our mental health.

Talk about the issues

As I've mentioned, the people around us may find our executive functioning difficulties confusing and frustrating (and they may be very vocal about this!). As awkward as it may feel, the best thing to do, depending on your life situation, is to talk about it. Explain to your friend, parent, boss or partner the difficulty you have and why you have this. Ask them to read this chapter (actually, the whole book might be helpful for some!). Ask for help. I have found that explaining the things I have issues with and asking for help, or even just compassion, has made a world of difference.

SELF-COMPASSION IN THE FACE OF EXECUTIVE FUNCTIONING DIFFICULTIES
Suzi

Self-compassion is so important, especially in times of stress. When we feel we have messed up in some way (e.g. because of our poor executive functioning skills), many of us develop a harsh inner critic that shames and blames us. We often put up with this voice and don't realize we can choose to change it to a kinder one. What? Yes, seriously. It's basically the protective part of our brain that is trying to keep us safe.

By keeping us doing what we've always done, it thinks that it's keeping us from harm. Well, my friend, here's the good news. Slowly, bit by bit, we can change our narrative.

A good place to start is by identifying the unhelpful thought. For example, 'I'm a terrible person because I forgot their birthday again.' Pause and ask yourself, how does this thought make me feel? I'm guessing something like annoyed, frustrated and ashamed.

Next question: 'How would I like to feel?' The answer might be, I'd like to feel OK and happy with myself. So, what thought or belief would be helpful in this situation? 'I'm sad I forgot her birthday. I have genuine challenges with memory. I will put it in my calendar (straight away).' How does this thought make you feel? I'm guessing better.

What else can you do to try to make sure you learn from this? Apologize and be honest and put their birthday on your calendar for every year, not just this year?

Then move on.

Reparenting yourself through executive functioning hacks

Many of us grew up in families that were antagonistic at best. If this is true for you, finding compassionate ways to manage your executive functioning issues is a must. By being kind to ourselves and finding ways of doing things that work for us, we are in a sense 'reparenting' ourselves.

As adults, we can give ourselves what we didn't get as children. Stop beating yourself up with that stick made from other people's old and outdated views about you. You know that you are intelligent and capable. If you need to pay someone else to wash your clothes, just do that. It's good self-care.

Suzi's thoughts on executive functioning
Break tasks down

When executive functioning is challenged, it can make it hard to break tasks down. One way to help with this is to start with the end/outcome in mind so that you know what you are aiming for, and note down all the steps to take to get to the desired outcome. For example, if the outcome is to 'Tidy the bedroom', the steps to take are:

- Clothes on floor – sort into 'clean' and 'needs washing'.
- Place dirty clothes in washing basket.
- Fold clean clothes and put in wardrobe.
- Change bedding – take bedding off and place in washing basket.
- Choose new bedding and put on bed.

By breaking tasks down, they can seem more manageable and having a plan/list can help with feeling in control as well as feel satisfying if you tick each action off.

Breaking tasks down can take a bit of time, but it can actually save time if procrastination gets involved and delays things even further. Also, much of the decision making has already been done, so when it comes to cleaning and tidying, it will hopefully feel easier. Plug in some music or a podcast and you're good to go.

This process can be applied to any task, and if you still find it difficult to break it down, then please find a trusted person who can help you. Some people love this stuff!

Coaching

Coaching can really help with executive functioning strategies, and with specific difficulties. Body doubling can also help you to get going and complete tasks. This is where you 'buddy up' with someone, either in person or online, and let each other know what you are working on, then you do it in the presence of each other. It is remarkably effective.

Be compassionate about working memory issues

Working memory can be impaired, and it can feel so frustrating when you can't recall something you literally just heard. I sometimes forget what I am saying mid-sentence which can be embarrassing! I have learned to accept that my working memory is a particular challenge for me and to try not to give myself a hard time when it fails me. It is not my fault after all. I would often feel shame when I forgot a friend's birthday or, worse still, their kid's birthday. These days I know that it's hard enough keeping up with birthdays and anniversaries, never mind kids' birthdays, too!

It's important to see that poor working memory is not a character flaw, a weakness or a reflection on you as a person. At times when your memory fails you, it can be helpful to come back to your truth and intentions – you didn't forget on purpose.

Remember, the challenges are very real but they can be helped. It may take a fair amount of trial and error before you find strategies that work for you, and that's OK. It's also worth remembering that what works for one person may not necessarily work for you.

Every person's brain is different and that includes us autistic folks. There is no one way to do things, only our way to do things. Have fun and experiment with different techniques.

The good news is that even if something does not work, the knowledge that that strategy does not work can be used as a learning experience.

— Chapter 5 —

Communication

SUZI

> *People who don't know me might think, 'Oh, you, you know, you're not very caring because you're really blunt and direct', where, actually, I care about everyone all of the time, but to the detriment of my own wellbeing.*
>
> LISA

You may have realized by now that autistic communication can be quite different from the neurotypical way. It almost seems like a different language and one that I have spent a lifetime learning! The key word here being 'different' and certainly not 'lesser', 'bad' or 'wrong'.

Autistic folk tend to communicate in a clear and direct way, and we basically say what we mean without any hints or expecting others to 'read between the lines' to decipher unsaid messages within the words used, which, let's face it, is downright annoying, confusing and unnecessary! 'Just say what you mean!' is what I have wanted to scream out thousands of times!

Alice said:

> Sometimes I wonder how different it would be to be autistic in a country with a language that is more direct like Germany or Holland. Or somewhere where people just say what they mean.

Because I know in England, we have a view of the Germans and the Dutch as being direct to the point of being rude. But as an autistic person, I think that just seems like it would be much easier.

So many misunderstandings happen due to differences in communication styles, which often result in the breakdown of relationships.

Us autistic folk tend to have a literal understanding of language, and this can result in a wide range of misunderstandings that can range from obvious to subtle and everything in between. One example of mine was when I was working. A colleague asked me to get her a chicken sandwich from a well-known bakery chain. When I got there, there was only a chicken baguette, no sign of a sandwich. My brain was confused. She had asked for a sandwich. For a while I was frozen and could not decide. The anxiety and self-doubt crept in. Should I just get the baguette even though she hadn't asked for it? What if it was the wrong decision? Eventually, I decided to get the baguette.

When I gave it to her, while over-explaining that they didn't have sandwiches only baguettes and apologizing if this was not what she wanted, she just looked at me in a confused way and said, 'That's what I asked for.' 'No, you didn't,' I wanted to say. 'You said "sandwich!"'

It took a while for me to recover from this misunderstanding because I used to think everything was my fault and that I was always getting things wrong. My thoughts would spiral downwards, and I would not speak to myself in a compassionate way. In turn, my feelings spiralled, too. Until I learned self-compassion and changed my internal narrative to that of a nurturing and supportive voice, I felt misunderstood pretty much throughout my life.

Many breakdowns in communication arise from neurotypical folk not realizing how literal autistic folk are at processing and understanding language. One area of ongoing confusion (for me anyway) is when people casually use an idiom in conversation. Not only can it cause confusion and sometimes embarrassment, but it can also cause a sensory response, too. Katharine highlighted this during her interview when she explained, 'I will interpret everything literally. And even those kinds of phrases that people use like "Oh, can I pick your brains?" make me feel sick. It even makes my head tingle. It's absolutely horrible.' I agreed and was reminded about another gruesome phrase, 'Keep your eyes peeled'. I have a highly visual imagination and that phrase does not bring a nice image to mind!

If you have felt misunderstood, too, then I want you to know that it's not your fault and it never was. So many late-identified neurodivergent folks have received so many messages throughout their lives that they are 'wrong' or 'not good enough' and are somehow at fault when communication breaks down. This will have led to their self-esteem and confidence being battered and to them feeling so low that it can be hard to see a way back up. The good news is that it is never too late to build your self-esteem and confidence! Once you know what has been going on and that there are perfectly valid reasons for the challenges faced and the misunderstandings that have taken place, you have the knowledge and power to make changes that serve you.

Something you can do right now to help is recognize the differences, notice them in action (without judgement if possible), especially when interacting with neurotypical folk, and be compassionate with yourself when usually you would give yourself a hard time. For example, thoughts such as 'What's wrong with me?' can be changed to 'I communicate differently and that is OK'. It might be helpful to remember that communication styles are different, and one is not better or worse than the other; they are simply different.

Other ways to help are to ask people to be clear and direct when talking/communicating with you as this is how you interpret and process language. In fact, this is such a big deal for me personally that I incorporated the message into my first ever comedy show at the Brighton Fringe festival and my alter ego Polly Parton (cousin of Dolly) wrote and sang a song to the tune of Tammy Wynette's 'D-I-V-O-R-C-E' called 'A-U-D-H-D you see' with the lyrics 'Clarity is good for me, so be mindful when you speak. I need you to be clear with the words that are coming out of your beak.'

THE DOUBLE EMPATHY PROBLEM
Kate

As autistic people, we can sometimes feel like we are literally speaking a different language from some of the people around us. In 2012, Dr Damian Milton developed a theory called the 'double empathy problem' to explain this phenomenon.

The double empathy theory states that there is a mismatch between the life experiences of autistic and non-autistic people. This difference can lead to a lack of mutual understanding and miscommunications, even about the most simple things, like talking about what we each did over the weekend.

It is called the 'double empathy problem' because the issues it causes with communication are two-way. The difficulty is mutual: the autistic person doesn't understand the non-autistic person and vice versa. The empathy bit has to do with the myth that autistic people lack empathy, which is not true. It is more the case that the level of empathy we experience is actually often much greater than that experienced by our non-autistic counterparts. It is also true that autistic people and non-autistic people express empathy in different ways.

It can feel as if, as autistic people, it is our fault that these conversations don't go well. However, it is vital that we see that it's simply a case of differing communication styles and not that we are doing anything 'wrong'.

> I find the best way to deal with these types of situations is to be straightforward and ask questions if I don't understand something. I'm also very kind to myself if I put a foot wrong. I try to see the funny side as much as possible!

More tips to pass on to friends, loved ones and colleagues/employers

- Please only give me the necessary information in clear and direct language.

- Avoid use of idioms if you can. If I have not heard them before or spent time finding out what they mean, I can become very confused, and this can lead to embarrassment when I don't know what you mean.

- Please be specific. If I ask if you can meet me tomorrow at 2pm please give a definite response and avoid ambiguity such as 'maybe' or 'should be able to'. Please respond as soon as possible so that I know what is happening and when. This helps me feel calmer and more secure in what to expect. (Note from Kate: I briefly dated someone who was proud of being 'reliably unreliable', and when asked if he would be somewhere at a certain time, he would say, 'I can give a definite maybe.' Needless to say, he didn't last long!)

- If verbally giving me instructions, then please give one at a time and allow time for me to process what you have said.

- Don't assume an autistic person will understand unspoken instructions. For example, if you ask them to put the washing in the tumble dryer, you may also need to tell them to turn the tumble dryer on.

- Say what you mean and do not assume I will pick up on unsaid messaging; for example, say 'Please open the window' rather than 'Ooh, it's hot in here, isn't it?' and then expecting me to pick up on what you have not said and open the window. The likely response to the latter will be 'Yes, it is hot'.

- Feel free to check my understanding by asking something like 'When do you need to have completed this by?'

- If I ask you to repeat something, please keep your face and tone neutral and repeat it at the same speed and volume as the first time. It is very hurtful and condescending when people speak louder and slow their voice down.

- Please follow up important information via email/text/preferred medium so that I can reference and process it later if I need to. This will also help me to remember what has been said.

- With written communication it is also important to be direct – mark out actions clearly, highlight deadlines and keep it as short and simple as possible.

- If you are flirting with me, you will probably need to back it up with clear and direct verbal information! I find it hard to recognize if someone is flirting, so if you ask me out to dinner, it would be helpful to add the words 'on a date' – otherwise, I may assume I am going to dinner with a friend.

- Please don't assume I have hidden meanings to what I say.

COMMUNICATION

If I say, 'There's a lot of washing up there', I do not mean, 'There's a lot of washing up and I think you should do it.' I was literally stating a fact. That's it, no hidden agenda.

- Only ask a question if you require an honest answer. If you are looking for compliments or reassurance that your new hairstyle suits you, be aware that an autistic person is likely (not always) to give you an honest factual response. You may not like the answer, but it is important to realize this is not a personal attack; it is the autistic person being honest. To say something that they don't mean or believe would feel like lying and, remember, one of my strengths is honesty, so please accept this.

- Please take time to ask me about my communication style and preferences. I have spent many years working out the neurotypical style of communication, and it's only right that we meet halfway and try to understand each other.

- Please be patient with me, and if I tell you I am struggling to express something or understand, then accept that this is my truth, even if you cannot see it.

- Please do not expect me to change who I am and to learn or use your preferred style of communication. Understanding and acceptance is a two-way thing.

- Please do not assume that I don't care if I don't respond in the way you expect. Often it takes me a while to process what I am hearing.

- Please don't read my facial expression (or lack of) and assume you know what I am thinking. My facial expression often does not match my thoughts and feelings, so just ask me.

- Be specific. The more specific you can be, the more likely I am to understand what is required.

- Ask me what works for me. Remember that each autistic person is different and no two autistic people are the same. Oh, and listen to what I say. Thank you.

Communicating with other humans can be difficult, confusing and often frustrating. Miscommunications and misunderstandings have been the cause of many meltdowns and shutdowns throughout my life.

As a determined, creative problem solver, I have spent hours, maybe even years, working out how to communicate with others in a way that serves me and honours my needs/wants and doesn't offend others. As I mention in Chapter 15: Passions and Interests, I have studied human behaviour since I was about 11 (no coincidence that was the time I started secondary school, when cliques were made and unwritten rules of friendships caused no end of upset and confusion).

Assertiveness is key

Something that has had a life-changing effect on the way in which I express my needs, wants and feelings has been learning how to communicate assertively. Assertiveness is not something that is only available to neurotypical folk, and it most certainly can be learned. It takes time, patience, awareness and practice, and can lead to improved relationships (at work and at home), increased self-confidence, better mental health and wellbeing as well as fewer meltdowns/shutdowns. Assertiveness skills can help us to deal calmly with conflict as well as to communicate our boundaries.

So, what does assertiveness mean?

Assertiveness is a tool we can use to get what we want and need in life. We can use it to advocate for ourselves and for others as well (e.g. our children or other loved ones). In her first book, Kate wrote:

> Assertiveness is a quiet power. It's a way to communicate honestly and respectfully to get what you want and need in life. Being assertive means respecting yourself by standing firmly by what you believe is right. You will gain the respect of others by not backing down.[1]

To put it into context, assertiveness sits between passive and aggressive communication styles, not forgetting the passive-aggressive style, which often manifests as gaslighting, sneaky hidden messages wrapped up in nice words, resulting in people appearing fake, narcissistic, sociopathic and so on.

Passive people generally do not speak up for themselves, don't express how they truly feel and let others take the lead. This was the main style that I presented with for most of my life up until about six years ago when I decided enough was enough and I was fed up with not feeling seen or heard.

Aggressive people tend to speak the loudest and insist that their way is the right way and that everyone else should follow them. Do previous (or current) managers come to mind? They don't consider other people's feelings and are often described as bullies and manipulators. If you resonate with this style of communication, please realize that everyone on this earth is doing the best they can with the skills they have. The good news is that new skills can be learned.

There are many reasons why people develop these communication styles, and many people are a mixture of all the above, depending on mood, environment and situation, to name a few factors. To delve into these reasons is beyond the scope of this book, so I am sharing a framework that I learned over 15 years ago that I still use now which has served me very well.

The four step process for assertiveness

1. Use the person's name.
2. State how you feel using 'I' statements.
3. State your reason for feeling that way.
4. Ask (confidently) for what you want.

An example of the process in action

Context: I was working for an educational organization and much of my day was spent in a small office with two other people. This suited me very well. However, the organization grew bigger, and we were all required to move and work from a large open-plan office.

The change unsettled me (and freaked me out). I was happy where I was, and the thought of being with lots of (possibly noisy) people filled me with dread. My first instinct was to get upset, raise my voice and declare, 'I am not working in a big office with lots of people.' I probably did say this to my immediate colleagues, who were also friends.

We visited the new office in our team, and I knew I had to sit in a corner space next to the wall and away from the noisy photocopier.

Using the four-step process, I said to my manager (who happened to be very nice, kind and understanding):

• Use the person's name.	Laura
• State how you feel using 'I' statements.	I'm feeling really worried about the possibility of working in the bigger open-plan office.
• State your reason for feeling that way.	It's because I find it hard to filter out noise and I worry that people will approach me from behind and make me jump.
• Ask (confidently) for what you want.	Please can I sit in the corner desk, and can the photocopier be located as far away from me as possible?

This process can be adapted for avoiding conflict in a calm and clear way, as well as during conflict where your needs/wants are not being acknowledged. It is worth mentioning here that I believe that 'most' people are doing the best they can with the tools they have got, and 'most' people do not deliberately seek to misunderstand and create conflict. Many people, neurotypical and neurodivergent, simply do not have the tools, understanding or awareness of themselves and others to go about every interaction with calm and grace.

An example of when boundaries are being crossed and you feel you are not being heard or understood

Context: This is a real-life example of mine when I worked as a teacher in a residential school and my duties were changed with no consultation and at very short notice. I was told to transport the students from Sussex to London on a weekly basis, and this was not part of my job description.

Notice that I used 'I' statements and feeling words. If I said what I 'really' wanted to say, then the outcome may have been different. What I really wanted to say was, 'FFS, you idiot, why the F do you keep sending me to London when my job is to teach? It's making my life at this school really difficult and making me want to leave.'

So, did I leave? Eventually, yes. This place was not right for me, and to be honest, I stayed far longer than I should have. Thank goodness I am out of there!

• Use the person's name.	Trevor
• State how you feel using 'I' statements.	I'm feeling really unhappy about being asked to transport the students up to London on a weekly basis.
• State your reason for feeling that way.	It's because it is causing me a great deal of stress as it is outside my usual routine.
• Ask (confidently) for what you want.	Please can this be an occasional request when no other staff are available, with as much notice as possible?

Do it your way

Remember, you have the right to communicate in a way that suits you. If you need to write an email, then do so. In fact, having an electronic copy is useful, not only for your own records but also for evidence if things become difficult and if you are not being reasonably accommodated in a job. However, caution is needed when writing an email/text in the 'heat of the moment' in case you say something you later regret. I often draft my email first and then come back to it later once I have calmed down and can amend it where necessary. Also, if you are anything like me and have memory issues, then having a record of conversations can be helpful to refer to and remind you of what you said and when.

— Chapter 6 —

Sensory Processing

SUZI

I feel like an exposed nerve in a world where everyone else lives in a shell and everything just hits me really hard.

HANNAH

Most autistic individuals have some sensory processing differences. We can be over- or under-sensitive to sensory stimuli. Both of these scenarios can cause stress and anxiety.

The senses can be a source of great enjoyment, awe and wonder, yet also of difficulty, overwhelm and stress. In this chapter, I'll discuss how the senses can affect everyday living as well as ways to bring the senses into balance so that life can be more calm, peaceful and enjoyable.

Self-awareness is critical if we are to understand our sensory needs and recognize when they are not being met so that we can do something about it. Many of us, me included, grew up not realizing that much of our stress and anxiety, let alone exhaustion, came from sensory overload/overwhelm.

Looking back on my 17 years of teaching, I can see how much I was affected by sensory overload at pretty much every turn. The noise, the hordes of students, the lights, the constant demands, the lack of breaks/time out, the fear of people touching my shoulder from behind to get my attention... The list goes on. Thankfully, now as a self-employed speaker, coach, comedian and trainer, I am able to design my day (and life) with the senses in mind and am grateful to be able to manage my energy in ways that I never have before.

It is worth noting that in the three years since becoming self-employed, I have only had about three meltdowns that I can recall, and the most recent was when I packed so many experiences into one week that my poor nervous system was overwhelmed. Throughout my teaching career, I can assure you that I had hundreds of meltdowns and burnouts.

Understanding your sensory profile

To work out what your sensory differences are and the effects they have on you, it's a good idea to create a way of tracking what is going on – especially if you are feeling tired/exhausted, are having meltdowns/shutdowns and are generally feeling 'frazzled'.

Methods for tracking could be journalling, spreadsheets, symptom tracking apps and so on. It is important to find a way that suits you. Talking with others can also be useful as the people closest to you may see things that you might not find obvious. Coaching or counselling may be helpful as well, depending on your needs.

HOW OVER- AND UNDER-SENSITIVITIES OF THE SENSES CAN IMPACT ON DAILY LIFE
Kate and Suzi

Sight (vision)
Over-sensitive: You may find images and video distressing; bright lights, distractions in the environment and/or busy environments may cause overload.

Under-sensitive: You might crave lights, glitter and busy visual environments. Taking in a lot of visual stimuli may be calming for you. ('This is 100% me!' says Kate.)

Sound (auditory)
Over-sensitive: You may be able to hear the buzz or hum of lights/machinery, and things like ticking clocks, clicking pens, babies crying and lots of people talking at once may be distressing. You may find it hard to focus on one person when you are in a group. Sleep may be difficult unless you have absolute silence.

Under-sensitive: You might need a lot of noise to feel regulated. You might prefer loud music and be drawn to novel sounds like voices with accents different from your own, or the 'boing!' of a door stopper. The washing machine spin cycle, hair/hand dryers or the sound of a vacuum cleaner may be calming.

Smell (olfactory)
Over-sensitive: Smells can be distressing and may cause a physical response. For example, you may gag, feel or be sick, and a strong smell may be so distracting that you can't focus on anything else. Things like washing powder, fabric softener, shampoos, soaps and lotions may be too strongly fragranced for you, and you might need fragrance-free options (for yourself and the people in your life, which may require some negotiation!). You may find environments where there are a lot of competing scents very difficult to manage.

Under-sensitive: You may not be able to smell something everyone else can smell; you may wear too much fragrance because you can't smell it. You might not be able to smell 'warning' smells, such as smoke, chemicals or when food has gone off.

Taste (gustatory)

Over-sensitive: You may find some textures very challenging, and you might prefer bland foods; you may only be able to eat 'safe' foods and may struggle when the recipe or packaging of a safe food changes.

Under-sensitive: You might love crunchy and/or highly textured foods and more strong and spicy flavours.

It's important to note that many autistic folks have experienced the trauma throughout their lives of being made to eat food that was genuinely revolting for them. It's also useful to note that our sense of taste is strongly linked to our senses of smell and touch, and there may be overlapping issues with these.

Touch (tactile)

Over-sensitive: Light touch may be distressing. You may need softer clothing and you may prefer seamless socks and underwear. You may need to cut labels out of your clothing.

Under-sensitive: Deep pressure may be more comfortable for you. You may love the feeling of different textures, vibration, massage, skin brushing and so on.

Vestibular (deals with balance)

Over-sensitive: You may have difficulty with balance, and walking on uneven ground such as cobbles or ice can feel very unsettling and unsafe. You may find it stressful to have your feet off the ground, and things like roller-coasters and high buildings may be challenging. You may struggle with stairs, and you may dislike spinning and movement in general.

Under-sensitive: You might love spinning, rocking, movement and high-intensity sports like bungee jumping or hang-gliding.

Proprioception (deals with body awareness, spatial awareness and the position of your head)

Over-sensitive: You may struggle to hold cutlery and/or writing instruments. You may have a 'stompy' walk which gives you more sensory feedback. You may stand or sit in what others feel are 'unusual' positions because this helps you to feel more calm.

Under-sensitive: You may not know where your body is in space. You might feel most comfortable when you are leaning against surfaces (or people). Suzi says, 'I often walk into chairs, tables and door frames and have so many bruises! I can laugh it off mostly, but at times I feel so frustrated and angry when I hurt myself "again".' Hannah explained her proprioceptive under-sensitivity this way:

> I can't feel the edges of my body... I can't feel where I am in space and where I begin and end...as soon as my muscles are relaxed, it feels like my body is floating away from me. It almost feels like I have to keep tense to keep myself together.

Interoception (how the brain interprets bodily sensations)

Interoception deals with bodily signals such as hunger, thirst and whether or not we need the toilet. It is very complicated and the over- and under-sensitivities can actually cross over, so we'll just give a general overview.

It's very important for us to understand how our individual interoceptive sense operates. We can run the risk of becoming dehydrated or malnourished because we don't know when to eat. We may wait far too long to use the toilet, or go to the loo very often 'just in case' because we don't know when we need to go.

Nociception (how the body interprets pain)

Over-sensitive: You may have a very low pain threshold and feel pain at the slightest knock.

Under-sensitive: You likely have a very high – or almost no – pain threshold. People with a very under-sensitive nociceptive sense run the risk of breaking bones or suffering serious internal injuries without realizing it. Loren told us that once he broke his foot and it took a long time to recognize this – he rode his bicycle and walked around on his broken foot for weeks. If you have been involved in any sort of accident and you know your nociceptive sense is under-sensitive, be sure to get checked out for broken bones and other injuries.

Thermoception (how the body interprets heat or cold)

Similar to interoception, there are crossovers between hot and cold under- and over-sensitivities. People with thermoceptive differences may not wear a coat in the winter or may enjoy touching very hot surfaces. It's important to note that the elements will still do damage (a person who doesn't feel the cold may still get frostbite).

Everyone's sensory differences are 100 per cent valid!

Many autistic folk who I speak to talk of having to set alarms to remind them to take a break, go to the toilet, drink water and eat. When I attend hospital or doctors' appointments, I have made it a habit to let the doctors know to ask me specific questions to help me focus my attention. Also, for me, 'How do you feel?' is a very vague and general question to which I might reply 'OK' even if I am in pain.

SENSORY PROCESSING

If I get too hot, I can start to panic, and often removing items of clothing is my go-to in this instance. If I struggle to remove the clothing – for example, if the cuff of my sleeve gets stuck – then my fight/flight kicks in, and before I know what is happening, I am having a panic attack. What helps me in these moments? Repeating the words 'I am OK' and 'I am calm' while deep breathing. Often, I can do this and avoid a panic attack; however, if I am in full-blown panic attack, then I breathe through it, know that it will pass and give myself permission to recover emotionally and physically afterwards.

I remember a time when I attended a training session and the trainer's breath smelt very strongly of garlic. It took all of my might not to gag when she spoke to me. Then the person I sat next to had a 'loud' rumbling stomach! The two sensory 'assaults' changed my emotional state, and I felt irritated throughout the session and could not concentrate. The effects of such experiences can last all day if not managed well, and in addition I had to 'be nice' and sociable, which was the last thing I felt like doing.

Unexpected touch is hugely challenging for me and many autistic people I have met, and leads to anxiety! Light touch can be distressing for some people, while others need deep touch. Remember, everyone's experiences are different, and it is your right to communicate your needs and boundaries. Even if people don't understand your individual differences, you still have the right to express your needs and wants and to have them respected.

It is important to remember that how you are affected by sensory differences is part of your reality and 100 per cent real and valid. I say this because it is common to have our sensory experiences denied, not believed, and misunderstood. There is still a lot of ignorance about sensory processing, and I always tell people in my autism training sessions that if an autistic person tells you that something is bothering them, you should believe them. Accept what they are saying and certainly do not say 'Everyone does that' or 'It's not that bad'. This type of comment has caused me so much trauma over the years as it is so invalidating!

No one will know exactly how you are affected by your senses and how they interact with the environment, and this is why self-awareness, finding ways to communicate your needs, having confidence to express them and managing your sensory input are so important.

Loren's sensory processing journey

When I was younger, I had a lot of sensory difficulties to the point where I would regularly shut down in public. I'd be stuck on a street corner, or on a bench, staring at the floor. But now as an adult, things are very different.

Yesterday I was on trains for probably eight hours. It was a strike day and I was going to South London, and the trains before and after the one I ended up getting on were cancelled. So, numerous trains, numerous cancellations, I was diverted. I was standing up for an hour, smushed between people. I was also teaching at a hospital for many hours. I can manage all of that now as an adult because I have a lot of control in the rest of my life.

My window of tolerance is quite wide. I've got a lot of control. I've got a lot of strategies and little routines. Also, noise cancelling is so easy now, with so many options for ear plugs and headphones. Of course, noise cancelling doesn't help you if you've got a stranger sweating on you on the train while you've been standing up for an hour...

I think driving has probably made the biggest difference, because now most of the time I've got my own controlled, contained environment. When I'm in the regular world, I can manage so much better because my window of tolerance is now so wide.

Even now, if I'm out with people or out in public, I may not use earbuds at all if I'm walking around. Or I may use the bone-conduction ones so I can have a background sound on, but I can still hear everything. So, my sensory processing has changed quite dramatically because my window of tolerance has grown so wide.

I used to wear tinted glasses but I don't really need them

SENSORY PROCESSING

anymore. I've got four days of work coming up in a conference centre with glaring lights above me, and I can manage that, whereas in the past, absolutely not. I'd get migraines constantly, or I'd be in pain or my eyes would hurt or other sensory things would become more jarring because I'd be worn out.

There's a knock-on effect as well on, on our internal senses, our interoception, and the way that connects to our physical and mental health. When somebody is in control of a lot of the sensory things, or they've reduced a lot of that 'noise' for themselves, then the internal sensory stuff is easier to pick apart, notice and figure out. And if you can pick that apart, you can take action. You can make sure you've eaten, you're hydrated, you've slept. Or if you haven't slept enough, then you know you need to have a calmer day.

Understanding sensory issues gives you a greater ability to self-regulate as well because now that the sensory stuff is sorted out, you can actually deal with some of the health things that are splintering off from it. So, for me, proprioception is a big one – that need to move. It creates a lot of [mental] noise. For some people, proprioception gives them muscle tension and aches and pains, which causes them to feel physical pain and to be tired, fatigued, restless and anxious.

So, I've cut down some of the sensory noise by the control I have over my environment. Some of that proprioceptive stuff, which probably used to wreck me growing up, is now less of a problem. I'm getting fewer of the physical and mental health effects of it. It's really hard to convey just how big the sensory stuff is and how making some of those smaller changes can cascade as one grows older.

A game changer for me was that I got a newer computer and because of an improved processor, weirdly enough, using my camera in a darkened room with the lights off is now the same brightness as my camera was before with the unpleasant lights on. Technology is solving all our problems!

What helps?
Noise/busy environments

In-ear earplugs have been an absolute must in the neurodivergent community to help with the noise in busy environments such as pubs and conferences. Lisa said about hers:

> They're just amazing. I've got two pairs, one I think are called the quiet ones that just drown out lots [of noise], but the other ones are designed for you to be able to still hear conversation and you can still hear people talking directly in front of you.

Nick told us that before he understood his sensory sensitivities, a trip to a garden centre would be incredibly stressful. Now he uses noise-cancelling headphones and listens to ocean sounds in these situations and this has been a game changer for him.

Jeff explained:

> I have always been sensitive to sounds and lights. When I got connected to the autistic community, I learned about being more proactive regarding my sensory issues and began using ear protectors. I purchased earplugs and some noise-cancelling headphones. Both have been really helpful, especially when leaving the house. I go everywhere with them.

So, try to alter or adjust your environment. Ticking clocks can be placed in a different room or have their batteries removed. Listen to white noise. Leave if possible. Take regular breaks, limit screen time, get out in nature.

Sights/visual distress

Ask for reasonable adjustments such as to be in a room that does not have fluorescent lighting or to work from home. Jeff works all day on a computer and he said:

As an adult, I have figured out ways of coping with some of these things, like setting the background colour of software programs to black and using white text. I was doing this decades before 'dark mode' became a thing. I have been lucky in that I have figured out many strategies that work well for me, mainly by trial and error.

If you need to add visual stimuli, try fairy lights, glitter lamps or an animated screen saver.

ALL ABOUT STIMMING
Kate

'Stimming' is short for self-stimulatory behaviour, and a 'stim' is a specific behaviour. Most autistic people have several stims. We use stims to express ourselves. We also use stims to help ourselves self-regulate, protect ourselves from overstimulation and to reduce anxiety. Some of us also use stims to help us stay focused.

There are three types of stims, and here are some examples of each:

- **Hand stims:** Playing with/pulling hair, picking at fingernails or other things, flapping hands, clapping, thumb sucking, snapping fingers, rubbing fingers together, playing with putty or fidget toys.

- **Body stims:** Rocking, head bobbing or banging, spinning, leaning on things, people or pets, flicking fingers in front of eyes, flapping arms/hands, tapping or slapping parts of the body.

- **Vocal stims:** Repeating words, screeching, groaning, humming, singing, mimicking sounds.

Is it a stim or is it a tic?

You may wonder if your behaviour is a stim or a tic, which might be indicative of Tourette's syndrome. A stim is a pleasurable behaviour that we are in control of – we choose to stim. A tic is compulsive and out of our control. However, here's where the distinction gets tricky because some complex tics can look and feel deliberate, even when they are not!

Use movement to self-regulate

We have a valuable resource in stimming as it helps us to regulate our nervous system and counteract other sensory input. There has been much shame around the need to move and stim, but we now know that it is an essential part of maintaining our energy. Hannah demonstrated the benefits of stimming when she said, 'I've taken on a master's degree, and if I go to lectures when I'm allowed to move and rock and move myself around, I don't get exhausted so quickly.' She added, 'There's more in me if I do these things to manage myself – there's more of me at the end.'

When delivering online autism/ADHD training, I make it very clear to attendees that 'allowing' folk to turn their cameras off in virtual meetings is providing a reasonable adjustment which enables people to move and stim freely, and reduces visual stimuli. This is something that you can ask for.

Kate says:

> Movement is an easy, accessible tool we can use to regulate our nervous system. It doesn't have to be anything formal, like a certain amount of daily exercise. It can just be a few minutes of bouncing on a gym ball or using some resistance bands. Similarly, vocalizing is a brilliant way to calm ourselves. Singing along to favourite music and humming are both calming, and if you can find a place where you can actually shout and scream (the car is great for this), this will help to reduce stress and get you to a regulated place.

Rest and recover

Be sure to build rest and recovery time into your day. If you have been in an environment that has drained you, and your senses are overloaded, it is essential to rest and recover as this can be the difference between functioning and having a meltdown or shutdown. For example, if I deliver my three-hour autism training, I make sure I don't book anything else on that day. It has taken me a long time to establish this personal boundary but it is so needed if I am to prevent energy crashes and meltdowns. The benefits are that by looking after myself and my needs, I am able to live a happy and healthy life where I have energy for the things I love to do and for spending time with the people I love.

We are all different, and it is important to find what works for you and accept what doesn't. Nikki talked about loving live outdoor music gigs but being unable to tolerate indoor gigs:

> With what's going on, the environment – being in an enclosed space with so many different noises and smells – is too much. However, I can go to Party in the Park in Hyde Park where it's an outdoor gig and I can stand where I want and there's fresh air, and I'm not overwhelmed by people and smells. If somebody is walking too close, they're in my periphery, and I can stop and let them go by.

On self-acceptance, Nikki went on to say, 'Some environments are just not good for me because they cause me so much anxiety and stress. I just have to accept that they aren't for me.' Nikki talked about big in-person events run by coaches she follows and how she wouldn't be able to attend even though she might like the look of them:

> It actually makes me cry when I watch the videos. I look at the videos and think, oh my God, they're having so much fun, it just looks amazing. I would love to be able to do that because I just think that it looks like such an electric environment.

It was with sadness that she has realized, 'I know I can't do it and there has been a part of me that's had to make peace with that.' She talked of having forgiveness for herself and the need to say, 'It's OK that you can't do it.' And to grieve those things. 'By doing that, I've been able to let go of beating myself up for not being able to cope in certain environments.'

Kate's thoughts on sensory processing

It may seem that it's only those who are over-sensitive to sensory stimuli who might struggle in life. However, people who need a lot of sensory stimuli can become stressed and anxious when their sensory needs aren't met.

I am, in general, a sensory seeker. I actually need a lot of sensory stimuli in order to stay calm and regulated. My home is full of glittery things, fairy lights, lava lamps and so on. I love vibration movement. I need sound of some sort almost all of the time. I've recently installed a networked speaker system in my flat so that I can have music in every room. Bliss!

I recently went swimming with my daughter and in the adjacent pool there was a water aerobics session taking place. The music was booming! I was surprised at how calming I found this. As you become more aware of your needs, it's useful to note how different environments affect you so that you can get more of what you need and less of what you don't like.

If I don't have enough sensory stimuli, I get bored, and the boredom leads to anxiety. Much more on this in Chapter 7: Emotions.

— Chapter 7 —

Emotions

KATE

> *I think it was because of those long years of wearing different masks, like the 'funny Rico', to cope with the fact that maybe I had emotions that I didn't want to face, and all of this trauma, that I only confronted them fairly recently.*
>
> RICO

Just as autism is a spectrum, the way autistics feel emotions varies widely. Some of us feel emotions deeply and intensely, and can differentiate between emotions in ourselves and the people around us. For others, emotions are felt on more of a flat, level plane. Others have alexithymia, which makes recognizing and understanding emotions very difficult.

I am in the camp of those who feel emotions in a big way. I first became aware of this in my thirties (before I found out that I am autistic), when I developed a fierce crush on a work colleague. I felt my attraction to this person as a powerful, almost painful, physical hunger. I could see and hear my desire for him in my mind as a set of high-voltage lights being turned on one by one, obliterating all other thoughts. While I had experienced strong feelings about people when I was younger, this was the first time I can remember feeling these things as both emotional and physical sensations.

Why do we struggle with emotions?

As undiagnosed autistic children, we would have been left to muddle through, with greater or (most often) lesser success in understanding and assimilating emotional regulation skills. It is unlikely that anyone taught you these skills, because it will have been assumed that you would just 'get it', as a neurotypical child would. Unfortunately, autistic children don't tend to learn easily by observing those around them; they need explicit instructions. Because of this, most of us will have suffered from a great deal of emotional dysregulation well into adulthood, picking up emotional regulation skills on a non-linear, trial-and-error basis.

It is true that for some of us, by the time we reach adulthood (and by this I mean around age 30, because we are each much younger in ourselves than our biological age), we have a fairly solid grip on emotions. Happy, sad and angry are the first emotions we understand as children. As we go through life, we experience, understand and assimilate more sophisticated feelings such as disappointment, jealousy and shame. We learn to differentiate between anxiety and excitement, despite the fact that these can feel very similar.

It can take us a lot longer to get there than our neurotypical peers, but we do find our way eventually. It is important to understand that, as adults, we can still struggle to name, define and describe our emotions, even if we feel them on an intense level.

If you have no idea what I am talking about...

If what I am sharing here makes no sense to you, don't worry. Some of us have an incredibly difficult time understanding and naming our own emotions and those of the people around us. At some point, you may have been made aware that this is atypical, but you didn't know what to do about it. If you find that you are struggling with understanding your emotions, there are ways to learn.

How can we learn to regulate our emotions?

As I've said, most of us learn how to manage our emotions as we get older. You will know if emotions are a problem for you. If you are having frequent meltdowns or shutdowns, or creating drama in your life, you may have some work to do with learning to regulate your emotions.

The first step in doing this is to ensure that you understand what different emotions feel like for you. There are books available about emotions or you can simply search the internet for 'what are different emotions' to get you started. Michelle said it was helpful for her 'to understand that I am a human with human emotions and they are valid and can be given names if it's useful for me. So, describing human emotion is really important.'

Once we have a fairly good idea about what emotions we are experiencing, we can then look at which ones are a problem for us. For example, anger can be an issue for many people, as it's not something we are ever taught how to manage. Anger can be especially problematic for women, because as girls we are taught to be nice and not make a fuss. If you know that when something makes you angry, you go from perfectly calm to volcanic rage within seconds, you will need to look at this.

For some of us, the emotion of love can be an issue. Love is a powerful emotion, and it feels great! If you are a person who falls in love very quickly, and this has led to difficulties in the past, you might want to think about how you can manage this for yourself.

To manage our emotions, we need to get to know ourselves and our emotional triggers. So, for example, I know that any email from the person at the council who is dealing with my daughter's education will give me rage. I've learned to read the email and not respond until the next day (or week!). This keeps my anger in check and makes it easier for me to respond in a calm and more productive manner.

Think about your emotions and how you feel you manage them.

Are any causing issues? It's important to address this to ensure that your emotions don't cause problems in your personal and working relationships.

It's OK to feel big emotions

If you are like me and know that you feel emotions in an over-the-top way, I want you to know that this is OK. People around us may not understand why our happiness is almost manic and our sadness is like the end of the world. Although these feelings may seem out of proportion to what is going on, they are valid and acceptable. Your big feelings might make some of the people in your life uncomfortable. This is OK, too. You are entitled to feel what you feel, in whatever way you feel it. Big emotions in themselves don't necessarily need to be managed. If, however, your emotions are causing problems in your life, you'll want to work on this.

Visualizing emotions

Last year, I went through a devastating breakup of a long-term relationship. The months prior to this were agonizing, as the situation between my then-partner and me had deteriorated irreparably. During this time, my emotions were all over the place. This man was the love of my life, and my feelings for him were intense, but I knew it had to end as there was no way for the relationship to move forward.

During this time, I found visualizing my emotions very helpful. What colour is the emotion? How big is it? Does it have a shape? Where does it live in my body? These questions were very helpful for me as I unpicked all of the things going on in my heart and head. I actually found that painting and drawing pictures of the emotions helped me to further visualize what was happening for me.

Write it out

Sarah told us that writing out her emotions really helped her to work out what she was feeling:

> I find it helpful to get out all the raw emotions and thoughts and purge them out on a page. I feel seen; I can acknowledge whatever is going on...it would be very hard to get that level of feeling seen from somebody else... So, really listening to yourself is so helpful, and as you write and get things out, you start to understand better what's going on. And what's really fascinating is that often as I start writing, I feel think, oh my god, this is gonna be like a J.K. Rowling seven-part piece, and it's sometimes just a few pages. I'm like, how did that feel so big in my head?

This is my experience, too, and Suzi mentions it in Chapter 9: Anxiety and Stress. I journal prolifically, especially during times of stress. Like Sarah, sometimes emotions and worries can seem huge in my head, but when I write them down, they might encompass just a few paragraphs. When I sit down to write, I take time to re-read the previous day's entry and I am often surprised at the level of insight shown in my writing. I have learned more about myself and have overcome more difficulties by writing than by speaking for countless hours to various (and expensive) therapists in the past. Writing is free and you can do it anywhere.

Physically writing with pen to paper (or even electronic pen to tablet) is scientifically proven to be beneficial, improving memory and processing skills.[1] However, even typing out your experiences on a laptop or the notes app on your phone may help you organize your thoughts and feelings.

The empathy myth

There is a damaging and pervasive myth that autistic individuals lack empathy. You and I know this is complete nonsense. The reality is that we often have far too much empathy. Something upsetting happens and we implode emotionally because it's too big to process. It might not even be something that's happened to us personally but the death of a friend's pet or parent, or a distant relative.

Miguel explained that some highly emotional events in his life made him realize that sometimes he experiences huge emotions as a vacuum, because they are too big to process:

> I actually feel so much because my life is in high definition all the time. I'm super sensitive to everything, but mostly I feel too much emotion, but then [I don't know] how to label that emotion or that I've actually felt it.

As children – again, this was a time when we truly lacked emotional awareness and regulation skills – this kind of reaction will have been regularly misunderstood. Some autistic children appear not to react at all to the death of a family pet or close relative. The adults around the child are unnerved by this; it is not 'normal' behaviour for a child to not be conventionally sad at these times. The reality, of course, is that the sadness is far too big for the child to cope with, so it is compartmentalized in their heart and mind. The sadness or upset has been put into an imaginary bomb-proof box and stored away deep inside them. Perhaps the box will come out weeks, months or years later. For some, these huge feelings are never safe to look at again, and so they stay deeply buried.

We do this as adults as well. The number of sympathy cards I've bought but not sent over the years is proof of this (as I mention in Chapter 4: Executive Functioning). The downside is that unless the other person or people involved know us well, we can come across as cold and uncaring. At these times it's important to be kind to yourself; you know that you are a good and caring person, and being misunderstood is not your fault.

Alexithymia

Some autistic people have alexithymia, a phenomenon which causes difficulty understanding emotions. People with alexithymia will find it hard to name emotions in themselves and others. They may still feel emotions intensely, but have difficulty interpreting and understanding what they are.

Some of us are like Miguel, who experiences powerful emotions but struggles to interpret them. On the flipside are those of us like Jeff. Jeff told me:

> When I was growing up, I identified with the TV character Spock from *Star Trek*. I was a huge *Star Trek* fan and loved the actor Leonard Nimoy's portrayal of the Vulcan. Like me, he enjoyed playing chess, he loved cats and he played a musical instrument. He was different from everybody else around him, which is how I always felt. Like me, he didn't understand human emotions in others and struggled processing his own. I felt as if I belonged with Spock on Vulcan, not here on earth.

Nick came to see that he is alexithymic after a conversation with his wife. She was explaining an intense emotional response she was having to some upsetting news about a friend. She told Nick that she was experiencing sadness as 'waves crashing through her body'. Nick found this bewildering:

> I looked at her and thought, 'What?!' So, I googled 'Do you get sensations with emotions?' and I found this picture chart of human bodies with heat maps of emotion and how each comes with a sensation. I thought, 'That's weird! What is that?' So, I now realize that when I say I'm *feeling* something, what I really mean is I'm *thinking* something, and that feeling doesn't come with a sensation. I can still feel happy and sad, but I don't get a physical sensation with it.

In Chapter 6: Sensory Processing, we discussed the interoceptive sense, which deals with bodily sensations. Some alexithymic individuals find that exploring this sense can help them unpick emotions. This is actually useful for all of us autistics, alexithymic or not. There is a growing number of professionals, including occupational therapist Kelly Mahler, who are doing great work in this area. Search the internet for 'interoception and alexithymia' to find out more.

MELTDOWNS AND SHUTDOWNS

A meltdown happens when a person is completely overloaded with emotion and/or sensory stimuli. A meltdown causes the person to lose control as they desperately seek relief from what they are experiencing. They may lash out, scream, cry, break things, bite things or hurt themselves and others. This is a very scary experience, especially as the person may not recall their actions and may experience huge shame once the meltdown has ended.

Shutdowns occur for the exact same reason but manifest in a very different way. A shutdown will involve the person becoming very quiet and often very still. They may try to become as small as possible, putting themselves into small spaces, such as under a bed or inside a wardrobe.

Whether it's a meltdown or a shutdown, the person will need time to recover from what has prompted the reaction. The recovery time will depend on the person and the intensity of the meltdown or shutdown.

There's no shame in having a meltdown or a shutdown. These are quite normal for autistic people. Many people find that as they get older and become more aware of their sensory and emotional triggers, meltdowns and shutdowns become less and less frequent.

> In her book *Strong Female Character*, Fern Brady[2] writes about having intense meltdowns where she would smash up furniture as a way to release huge emotions. She has since learned to manage emotions and so no longer has these kinds of meltdowns. If you find that you are experiencing huge emotions that require almost violent physical release, you'll need to find ways to safely manage this.

Are you a drama or anger addict?

In my twenties, I went through a long period of huge, daily stress. Looking back on that time, I seemed to go out of my way to make my own life more difficult. I would spend all of my money, leaving myself unable to cover my rent and bills. I picked fights with my partner at the time, who was also a high-stress, volatile person. I would cause issues at work by leaving things until the last minute. Why did I make life so hard for myself? It took me over a decade to recognize that I did this to create drama, because drama makes me feel alive.

For some of us, emotions and physical sensations need special attention. This is especially true for those of us who are avid sensory seekers (more on this in Chapter 6: Sensory Processing). I am one of these people. I love (and literally need) bright, colourful lights, strong fragrances, big flavours and deep pressure. These things help me to feel grounded.

What I know about myself is that if I don't provide myself with what I need from a sensory perspective, I may create drama to get it. I can explain it best this way: the stress caused by a lack of money, being late or forgetting something important causes a rush of adrenaline and cortisol. Adrenaline creates physical sensations like a fast heart rate, sweating and dizziness. For those of us who are prone to creating drama, if we are not careful, we can become addicted to these sensations and cause all sorts of havoc in our own lives.

The same can be true for anger. If you are a person who is often starting arguments, fiercely complaining about this, that and the other or road-raging like a champion, you might want to have a look at this. Anger also stimulates a release of adrenaline and cortisol in the brain and the same physical sensations mentioned above.

Sometimes, we create situations that cause drama or anger for one huge but easy-to-overlook (and fix) reason: we are bored. If you are a sensory-seeking person, you need to provide yourself with a rich sensory diet of rewarding sensations. A sensory diet is nothing to do with food; rather, it is a set of activities you can engage in to help keep yourself regulated.

You'll want to ensure that you regularly provide yourself some of these things:

- flashing fairy lights
- glitter lamps or lava lamps
- aromatherapy – essential oils, diffusers, candles, and so on
- wearing fragrances
- exercise that uses big muscles and/or raises the heart rate
- massage, either by another person or yourself
- vibration
- exciting experiences
- snapping your wrist with an elastic band
- chewing gum
- a sauna or sauna blanket
- hot baths
- skin brushing
- orgasms
- spicy food
- crunchy food
- music.

The sensory-emotion crossover

It's useful to note that there is a strong correlation between our sensory processing needs and our emotions. Sensory processing and emotions also play a part in our levels of anxiety and stress.

Making sure that you have regular access to the things you require on a sensory level will help you avoid using powerful emotions as a way of getting your sensory needs met. Understanding your emotions will also help you to determine how you can use more or fewer sensory stimuli to stay calm and regulated.

Chapter 8

Masking

KATE

> *I moved primary schools when I was like nine or ten, and at the new school I was a completely different person... Looking back at it, it's clear something didn't work at my old school, so I changed and adapted to be who I thought would be more accepted. And I just think, how does a nine- or ten-year-old know to do this?*
>
> LAUREN

Masking is a survival strategy for autistic people. It is a way for us to appear 'less autistic' if we don't feel it's OK to be ourselves. In fact, at its heart, masking is driven by a person's belief that they are not good enough just as they are. Masking provides an opportunity for a person to become someone entirely different to their true self, chameleoning their way through life. In effect, they are hiding their true self because they believe there is something wrong with the way they are naturally.

Everyone, autistic or not, engages in masking of some sort. For example, if a person is anxious about a meeting at work, they may put on a brave face to get through it. For autistic people, masking is far more intense and it's nearly constant. An autistic person may mask every time they are in a social situation, while a non-autistic person only does it some of the time.

How did it start?

I can't remember a time in my life when I wasn't masking. It was made clear to me very early on in my life (around age two or three) that it wasn't OK to be myself (playful, curious, creative, questioning) and that my family would like me much better if I were someone else (quiet, 'good', 'nice', accommodating – even when this made me uncomfortable).

Katharine had a similar experience:

> I learned from a really early age that what I was and what people wanted of me were two very different things. And so I pursued the avenue of what people wanted from me really heavily to the point of just almost disregarding myself and who I was.

Even as small children, we understood cause and effect. We found that if we behaved in a certain way, people wouldn't engage with us, but if we behaved in a different way, they would. Thus, masking began.

Here are some examples of what this might have looked like for us as children and teenagers:

- Hugging a relative when we didn't like to be touched.
- Eating foods we hated or that made us feel sick.
- Enduring loud/smelly/visually busy environments when this was very stressful for us.
- Studying our peers to work out what they were talking about, wearing, interested in and so on, and then copying these things.
- Agreeing to do things that made us uncomfortable.

As adults, masking still looks like this but encompasses more grown-up stuff:

- Going to a job interview and playing the role of the person

who can do the job we are interviewing for (when we have no experience of this).
- Agreeing to do all sorts of things we don't want to do, from attending a social event to having sex with someone we don't fancy.
- People pleasing, in general.
- Becoming a completely different person when we change jobs or begin a new romantic relationship.
- Extreme perfectionism.
- Taking on the interests, traits and mannerisms of others in order to fit in, either with a single person or a social group.

Why do we do it?

As I've mentioned, at the core of our masking is the belief that we are not good enough and that something is wrong with who we naturally are. Masking also serves specific purposes in our lives. What follows are some examples of why autistic adults use masking.

To fly under the radar

An autistic child who lives in a volatile household or has a volatile teacher may mask to make themselves invisible and to keep the peace. This behaviour will become deeply entrenched to the point where it is part of them as a person. As an adult, this can lead to not speaking up for themselves and generally avoiding conflict, which can cause huge issues in their personal relationships.

To not 'look autistic'

Many of us are well aware of the ways we are different to the general population. We may hide our gorgeous, vibrant, autistic selves away in order to look 'normal'. More on this later.

To make friends or impress a potential partner

Masking makes us the best friend and partner ever! We might do whatever the other person wants, take up their interests, go where they want to go. This is impossible to keep up for very long. It can also put us in situations that are dangerous or that go against the grain for us, morally. (More on this in Chapter 13: Friends, and Chapter 14: Love and Sex.)

To get on with what we need to do

Similar to flying under the radar, masking and avoiding confrontation helps us to concentrate on work or something else we are trying to get done.

To achieve a specific goal

Masking can be a useful 'fake it till you make it' tool. I rarely mask these days, but I find it does come in handy for some work situations. For example, I recently had to deliver some in-person training (a post-pandemic rarity for me). I was not nervous about the actual training, but I was extremely anxious about getting there on time and parking. I masked my way through it, pretending this was no issue for me. This helped me get there and park up, and I delivered some of the best training I'd ever given.

Nick said, 'I think to an extent some masking has value as long as you are aware you are doing it. You have to recognize the benefits and deal with the consequences.'

This can be a positive aspect of masking, as long as it is only for a very finite, specific purpose. Whenever we consciously mask, we must factor in recovery time afterwards.

To please people in our lives

Here are some scenarios a masking adult may find themselves in. These kinds of situations can cause huge stress and have a deep impact on our mental health:

- If I know my partner gets annoyed when I need time to

transition from work mode to home mode, I may mask to pretend I don't need this in order to keep them happy.

- If my friend wants me to meet up with a large group of people, I may mask and do that (even though I can't cope with groups) in order to keep them happy.

- If my boss wants me to sit in a big, open-plan office and I find this incredibly stressful, I'll mask and pretend I'm fine with it as I don't want to annoy my boss.

I could go on and on here. If you find yourself masking to keep the peace, I advise that you look at areas where you can make changes. There may simply be no way round your current situation other than to mask your way through. If this is the case, remember my previous point about allowing for recovery time from the masking.

Because society tells us to
Autistic people mask because society tells us that being autistic is a bad thing. This is a sad fact but very true. The media tells us to embrace our true selves, but society doesn't really want that. Society loves conformity. Autism and conformity are not happy bedfellows.

How do we do it?
Masking isn't just one thing or another. We mask in all sorts of different ways.

Scripting and rehearsing conversations and jokes
Sometimes the material for this kind of thing comes from television or films, so the potential for getting it wrong is high as we may not understand the context of the conversation and try to apply one conversation to a wide range of situations.

Emma said:

I'll come up with a story to tell somebody, something that they'll think is funny. Everyone thinks I'm really funny, but that's because I've told the story in my head [over and over again]. That's like my main thing that I do, that everyone thinks I'm really funny because I'm always acting, putting on a show kind of thing. And then when I get home, I just don't speak to anybody and I just crash.

Playing past conversations over and over in our heads to find ways to improve in the future

We are extremely hard on ourselves. This is most apparent in social situations. From a few words exchanged with someone on the till at the grocery store to a long conversation with a friend, if we believe we've got something wrong, we can get extremely hung up on what we said and how we said it.

Of this, Hannah said:

> I used to store little memories in my mind of times when I just hadn't got it, when people had laughed at me or been cross with me, and I just had no idea why. And I'd lie in bed at night picking over them, and it might be something from years ago. What was it? What did I do that was wrong or what didn't I do, how did they know [that I'd got it wrong]?

We feel the need to ensure that whatever went wrong never happens again, so we ruminate over these exchanges for a very long time, analysing every word, our tone of voice and even our facial expressions. This is very stressful and totally unnecessary, especially as the other person likely didn't think anything of the conversation and it's just us agonizing over it.

Memorizing social scripts in order to engage appropriately in 'small talk'

Autistic people are very efficient. Small talk to us is like wasted air. However, we know that it is part of society and unless we can take part, we may look odd or rude. So, we may memorize standard small talk fare. For example, 'What did you do at the weekend?', 'The weather is terrible (or lovely), isn't it?' and so on. We also memorize reasonable answers in case someone asks us questions like this.

Researching topics we think might appeal to the people around us
Current events, popular music, television shows, books and films are all in this box.

Studying others around us in order to copy every detail (and fit in)
These days, what people are meant to wear to work and how people are meant to act at work are widely open to interpretation. When I was working in office situations (before I knew I am autistic), I found it extremely hard to work out how to be. The dress code was often given as 'smart casual', which meant nothing to me. I would study all of the women to figure out what to wear. I would focus on who seemed most liked and try to emulate that person, even if they were very different from me. I never got any of this right and it was very stressful.

The trouble with copying others is that how people dress and act are nuanced things with unspoken reasons and meanings. It takes relentless studying and practice to get these kinds of things right. The bottom line is, there's really just no need to do this.

Forcing eye contact
Eye contact is a hotly debated topic. Unfortunately, many people hold the opinion that if a person is not making eye contact, it means that they are not listening, and thus they are being rude. Many autistic people find eye contact extremely uncomfortable. I am one of these people. I prefer instead to look at someone's forehead. I have an audio processing delay, so sometimes I look at

their mouth as this provides a bit of lip reading that I find helpful. Ironically, for many of us, making eye contact makes it difficult for us to take in what the other person is saying. If you are a person who finds eye contact difficult but you are still making lots of eye contact, this is a sign that you are masking.

Not expressing sensory discomfort
Masking can look like not asking for reasonable accommodations at work or elsewhere – for example, not asking for fluorescent lights to be turned off, not asking a colleague to turn down their music, not wearing more comfortable clothing, not asking someone not to wear a strong fragrance and so on.

Not engaging in or talking about passions
We may have an intense interest in something that is not mainstream, but we have learned that talking about this seems to annoy or bore others, so we don't talk about it with anyone. If the passion or interest upsets our nearest and dearest, we may stop engaging in it altogether (see Chapter 15: Passions and Interests for more on this).

Not stimming
As mentioned in Chapter 6: Sensory Processing, stimming is short for 'self-stimulatory behaviours'. We all have stims. I rub my top lip and rub my fingers together. I also am a keen hair twirler. Stims are calming activities that can we engage in to keep ourselves calm and regulated. If we worry our stims are unacceptable to those around us, we may not engage in them, which can cause problems. Or we may find a less satisfying stim, such as chewing gum instead of thumb sucking, in order to ensure that those around us are more comfortable with our behaviour.

Jeff told us, 'There were stims that I did when I was growing up that I stopped doing because I was made fun of, and I wanted to fit in. Now I enjoy rocking from side to side or using one of my many stim toys.'

Working really, really hard to fit in

When we don't feel as if we are acceptable just as we are, we might do all sorts of things just to fit in. Here are some examples:

- Taking on hobbies or sports we have no interest in.
- Listening to music we don't enjoy.
- Watching television shows we don't like watching.
- Going to places we don't want to go to.
- Wearing clothing, shoes and/or makeup that makes us uncomfortable.
- Hugging people when touch is uncomfortable for us.
- Spending time with people we don't like.
- Doing things that go against what we believe in.

What's wrong with masking?

Masking can have some benefits, but the drawbacks are far greater. For starters, masking:

- is exhausting
- might put us in situations – sometimes even dangerous ones – we don't want to be in just to please others
- stops us from working out what we want and like
- can cause huge problems in friendships, relationships and work situations because it's hard to keep up on a long-term basis
- stops us from being ourselves and truly enjoying life
- may make it difficult to get an autism diagnosis because we don't appear 'autistic enough'
- may make it difficult to get adequate medical care as it may appear our concerns are not great enough to warrant treatment or medication.

BURNOUT IS REAL

Masking is like playing a role in a play all day, every day. The masker is always 'on', always being someone they are not. This is totally exhausting and enervating. When a person masks at a high intensity for too long, they will burn out.

> [After a full-on week at work] I may still go out, I may still meet with friends. I may still get even more depleted by not having that 'me time' and not recognizing that I needed that kind of time to just do what I need to do. Now thinking back, I did have duvet days as well, where I just thought, 'OK, I feel a bit flu-y.' I felt as if I couldn't move and I thought, 'I'm getting the flu', but then after two days I was fine. And it makes sense now that maybe I was just completely burnt out – that kind of autistic burnout. (Miguel)

Burnout makes a person feel that they are beyond exhausted. They are unable to do much of anything. They may even be unable to get out of bed or leave the house. Activities that would usually hold their interest no longer do. They may become depressed and irritable. Sensory sensitivities will become more pronounced. For some people, basic tasks become a struggle.

The only thing to do for burnout is to reduce all of life's demands, have a deep rest and stop masking. This may require leave from work or cancelling plans.

If you are in a place of burnout, you need to be very kind to yourself and allow yourself to take a break from as many demands and responsibilities as possible, until you begin to feel better.

Are you masking?

Here is an exercise to help you work out when and where you are masking (I can almost guarantee that you are, even if it's just a little bit):

- Either mentally or on paper, make a list of all of the activities you regularly take part in. These will include work, social activities and day-to-day things like shopping and commuting.

- Have a look at the list and think about how you feel when you take part in each of these things. Something like commuting should feel fairly neutral, while a social activity may make you feel happy or anxious.

- Next, think about how you feel after the activity is finished. For example, you might feel OK at work but totally wiped out when you get home.

- Once you have done this, make a list of all of the people in your life. This will include family, friends, colleagues and possibly service providers such as a therapist or coach. It might be that you spend in-person time with them, or virtual time via FaceTime, Zoom or other video messaging services, or they may just be people you text or phone regularly.

- Now, just as you did with the list of activities, look at this list of people and think about how interacting with them makes you feel. Pay close attention to your gut feelings about each person. Is there anyone on your list who makes you feel uneasy? Are there people on the list whom you feel you have to go out of your way to please?

- If feelings are difficult for you to identify, what are your thoughts on each activity and person? Are your thoughts positive or negative?

This is not a foolproof exercise and won't work for everyone, but it may give you a steer on where and with whom you are masking.

Who are you, really?

I feel the greatest tragedy with masking is that we come to a point in our lives where we don't have any idea who we are. We've spent decades emulating other people, which has stripped each of us of our true personality.

This is a very common thing for autistic adults. It was certainly true for me, and Katharine had this experience as well. She told us:

> I hit my thirties, and I kind of felt that I suddenly had this quite scary feeling that there was just a kind of void almost at the centre of who I was and that I didn't know who I was. It sounds really strange, but it was really quite terrifying.

Nikki said, 'What many people I think will probably observe about masking is that the later you are diagnosed, the more parts of yourself you have compromised and suppressed and become disconnected from.'

So, there's a job ahead of figuring out who you are and what you actually like, which we cover in Chapter 16: Getting to Know Yourself.

How to stop masking

Once you have identified some things you are doing and people you are giving your time to that are causing you to mask, you will have some difficult decisions to make. Generally speaking, if we want to stop masking, we need to stop doing the things and spending time with the people that make us feel we need to mask in the first place.

The challenge here is that it might be your job that is causing you to mask. Or it might be your partner. Or your mother. How do you just stop engaging with these things and these people?

The best thing to do here is to go for the low-hanging fruit. Go back to your list and look at the easy things to stop doing or the people with whom you can stop engaging. For me, this was spending time in social groups (as I prefer seeing people one to one) and cutting out a few people who just made me feel 'icky' (for lack of a better word).

Katharine's advice here is to be kind to yourself and not beat yourself up for masking up to this point. Look at little things you can change – perhaps you could stop making eye contact? Try things like fidgeting in a meeting when previously you might have kept yourself still. These things are not self-indulgent but ways to make yourself feel more comfortable.

Sometimes eliminating masking requires drastic action and enormous courage. If it is your mother or your partner who is the main instigator of your masking, you will need to figure out what you can do about this. Can you reduce the time you spend with or talking to your mother? Can you communicate with your partner about what's happening? Sometimes there's nothing for it but to leave a job or end a relationship.

Obviously, these are not quick and simple things to do, so be kind to yourself and take your time if this is what is needed. See Chapter 16: Getting to Know Yourself for more on this.

Reducing masking requires setting boundaries

In order to stop masking, we have to learn to stand up for ourselves. We have to put boundaries in place to protect our emotional, psychological and physical safety.

Prolific neurodivergent author and autism advocate David Gray-Hammond shared in his Facebook reel, *Boundaries are really important*:

> If you are a neurodivergent person, chances are that boundaries are something that you really need in your life, but you feel you

are not allowed to have those boundaries. So often when we're neurodivergent we're taught that our existence is for the benefit of others, for the comfort of others. The truth is that the people who disrespect your boundaries are the exact reason why you need to have them. Without those boundaries, your wellbeing is going to decrease on a daily basis. Neurodivergent people have a right to engage with the world on their terms and it's not fair to force them into another person's worldview or concept of how the world should be managed and interacted with.[1]

Exactly. We have a right to set boundaries to protect ourselves. This means saying 'no' a great deal more often than we may have done in our lives before now.

Setting boundaries can feel uncomfortable at first. Little and often is the best way to start with this. Say 'no' to things that don't hold an emotional charge, like a work do or shopping with a friend. Once you feel comfortable with these smaller boundaries, move on to more difficult scenarios like saying 'no' to the Sunday family lunch or a friend's wedding that you know you won't be able to cope with.

It will be hard, but you can do it. I have faith in you.

DO MEN MASK?

There is a myth that only autistic girls and women mask. It may be that autistic females are more likely to mask. I believe this is because, practically from birth, we are told to be accommodating, nice, good, non-fuss-making individuals. So, we have to hide our true feelings, beliefs and even morals and values in order to please some of the people in our lives. Even if we were not taught this by our primary caregivers, society and the media make this message very clear. It may be the case that more females mask than males, but it's more likely that women and girls simply mask in a different way from their male counterparts.

Men definitely mask! Just as girls are taught to be nice, boys are taught to be tough. A man may mask to hide a mental health issue that he feels may make him appear 'weak' to those around him.

You are brilliant just as you are

As I mentioned, our core belief that we are not good enough lies at the heart of why we mask. There may be situations where you feel you have to cover up your real self in order to be more acceptable to others. The truth is that you don't need to do that.

You don't have to please anyone but yourself. Of course, we are obligated to jobs, children and possibly elderly parents, and we want harmonious relationships, which requires compromise. However, you do not need to be anyone other than yourself in order to find happiness and contentment.

Nick and I talked a lot about masking in our interview. He told me that he's been reading about stoicism, and that an aspect of this is not caring what other people think about you. He said:

> That's really resonated with me because...the problem I'd had as an autistic up until that point was that I always cared what I thought other people thought of me, because I never felt I fitted in. Now that I know I'm autistic and I've happily accepted it, I don't care that I don't fit in and actually I really don't want to. So that's been a major mind shift in terms of my own settled happiness.

How do you feel about being autistic?

Nick touched on something here that is vital in terms of looking at masking and why we mask. As I mentioned, a lot of masking can be about looking 'un-autistic'. In order to be truly happy in and with ourselves, we need to embrace our autisticness.

In other parts of the book, we touch on the shame we can feel about our autistic differences and our inability to do things that seem simple to others. We also talk about how society and the media consistently feed us the idea that autism is a bad thing. We can get so bogged down in the glass-half-empty part of being autistic that we forget that the glass is also half full.

The thing is, all of the things that make you autistic are some of the things that make you *you*. There's nothing wrong with you. You may have challenges. You may have a lot to learn about yourself in order to make those challenges less challenging. You are still a wonderful person.

Suzi's thoughts on masking

Since I realized I am autistic at the age of 31, I have reflected a lot on my life and how I have learned to mask. I would say I am an expert masker, and although I didn't realize what was happening, I carefully observed those around me and became a version of myself that I was not always comfortable with.

For me, masking has been about putting the needs of others before my own and covering up who I truly am, as well as denying my needs (and wants) to appease others, to fit in and avoid people being annoyed at or disappointed in me.

It was exhausting! I use the word 'was' because I am now in a much better place emotionally and am able to honour and respect my needs and who I truly am. It honestly feels liberating!

One of my earliest memories of masking was when I started a new primary school at age eight and a girl said to me, 'You've got a really deep voice, haven't you?' I was mortified! 'What's wrong with my voice?' I asked myself. The fact that I immediately interpreted this comment as something 'wrong' with me is also very telling about how I grew up interpreting the language of others literally.

I now know that my voice was the flat monotone that people often talk about in relation to autism. I know this because when I am stressed, tired, overwhelmed or heading for a meltdown, my voice takes on the same tone.

This comment was to have a great impact on how I saw myself and behaved. I learned to change the pitch and tone of my voice to ensure that no one would ever make a comment like that again. I was literally trying to control what others said by changing part of who I was. It saddens me now to think about this, but it also gives great insight and understanding into how I became an expert masker over the years.

Another comment that led me to mask my true self was 'Cheer up, it might never happen'. For goodness sake, why do people have to make such judgements about other people's facial expressions? When someone said that to me, I believed that there was 'something wrong' with my facial expression. I worked hard to smile when around others or at least to have a look of calm and happiness about me. I confess, I still do this now, and there is still part of me that dreads those six words. However, now that I know what is going on for me, I do sometimes script a reply in case anyone says anything, such as 'I am fine thank you' or, depending on how my mood is, 'I do not need to smile to make you feel better, thank you.' Fortunately, I haven't needed to say either of these things as no one has said it to me for years, but the fear is still there, lurking in the depths of my psyche.

I am thankful that there is more understanding and awareness of how autistic folks' facial expressions are not necessarily an indication of their mood, but there is still a long way to go, isn't there?

Another way I masked over the years was to put up with or cover up when I was really bothered by sounds/noise. Sometimes a person will laugh out loud and the pitch will literally hurt my ears, and it takes all of my might not to cover my ears, give them a glare or leave the situation. This is a really difficult one to manage because it can be a hard conversation to have when another person's laugh causes you pain.

If I can remove myself from the situation, I will. For example, if I am in a pub and the laugh is coming from a nearby table, then I will speak up and ask whoever I'm with to move. It may feel like an inconvenience, but the alternative is worse – sensory overload, change in emotional state, not being able to be fully present and a possible meltdown.

This is one example of why it is so helpful to be able to advocate for and express your needs, which for me is also a part of unmasking. We cannot, however, be responsible for how others react to these needs, and this is why it is essential to surround ourselves with understanding people who listen, accept and believe what we say about our truth, our reality.

Another way I've masked has been laughing when I felt hurt, upset or insulted and pretending I was OK when inside I was anything but. I've also been in situations where I've changed my words because I had been laughed at for using big or technical words. I do believe that although this is not a great thing to do as I essentially played small and diluted my extensive vocabulary, it has helped me to communicate with many different people as I am able to talk to people and relate to them whether they are age five, ten, 15 or 80, and that is one of my strengths, so for that I am grateful.

Masking can lead to unhappiness, mental health issues, burnout and a sense of not belonging in this world. It is not helped by the society in which we are living (and breaking free from bit by bit) that tells us that we 'just need to get on with it', to 'not make a fuss', and to 'work hard' at any cost. With this conditioning, we soon pick up the message that our feelings don't matter as long as everyone else is happy.

This is compounded by comments such as 'you're so dramatic', 'it's not that loud', 'I can't smell anything' or good old 'cheer up' to name a few. It's not surprising that we cover up our true selves and needs, is it?

I KNOW WHAT MASKING IS AND I'M UNRAVELLING MY EXPERIENCE. WHAT NOW?

Many of my coaching clients say they don't know how to unmask and are confused about whether they are masking or not and what it even means to them. This is understandable. It's a confusing and vulnerable time when you find out you are autistic. I say it takes time to work out who you are and to try not to put too much pressure on yourself to figure it all out at once because that just isn't possible.

Learning to unmask is about getting to know yourself and finding out who you really are, what you really want and, of course, what you need.

A good starting point could be to think about/journal/talk about what masking means to you because it can mean different things to different people.

Sometimes masking can serve a purpose and you might choose to (or unconsciously) do so when the occasion fits, and that's OK. It's important not to get caught up in the 'shoulds' because of what other people are doing. When we first find out we are autistic, it can be very overwhelming (and liberating), especially when we read or hear of others' experiences and we naturally compare their experiences to our own. The danger here is that if they don't match, then we can start to doubt ourselves all over again.

Unmasking takes courage, self-awareness and understanding. It takes time, space, grace and compassion for the self. If you choose to unmask, then please be mindful of who you trust to see the true you. Remember that those close to you may struggle with the changes they see in you and not react in the most favourable way. If this happens, remember that it is about them and not you. We can only control how we act and behave, and not what others think, say or do.

Part of unmasking for me (even though I discovered that I am autistic over 15 years ago and am still figuring this stuff out) is to be confident to honour my needs and speak up if they are not being acknowledged. This takes courage and bravery, too.

Recently, I was at a meetup with other entrepreneurs when a group of mums and their toddlers entered the quiet cafe. The noise immediately triggered my sensitive nervous system and hearing. I felt a sense of panic creep up from within, and in that moment, I made the decision to speak up and tell the group that I would need to leave or sit outside because of the noise.

The group were all very happy to sit outside, which incidentally was quite chilly so we all zipped our coats right up and enjoyed the fresh air. I was so grateful to the group that they listened to me and accepted that I was struggling with the noise, and, without any fuss, honoured my needs.

Not every experience of unmasking will be or has been so positive, but it is a reminder that being around the 'right' people who understand you and don't judge is an absolute game changer on the journey to unmasking and becoming your true, unapologetic self.

Unmasking and being your true self is scary and it's such a vulnerable thing to do – though also liberating and empowering. Be aware that fellow humans love nothing more than to give their opinions and advice, especially when you don't ask for them, and as I mentioned before, they may feel uncomfortable with the change they see in you (because it will mean changes for them too), and often to ward off these feelings of discomfort that they are experiencing, they may say all sorts of unhelpful things. Remember, that is about them and not you.

It can help to remember your truth, who you are and all you have journeyed through to get to where you are today. You really are a remarkable human who is on a journey to self-discovery and all the excitement and wonder that this could bring.

You have most likely spent a lifetime covering up your true self to make others feel comfortable and now it is time to put yourself first, to recognize your worth and know that you matter.

— Chapter 9 —

Anxiety and Stress

SUZI

I'm very anxious. I must have been this way all my life because I can remember that I went on an away camp when I was about eight or nine and they would give a certificate to every child. I got a certificate for 'panicking'.

ALICE

It's a sad fact that you can't really talk about autism without talking about anxiety and stress. However, before we dig into the depths of the difficult topics of stress and anxiety, please realize that these are not something you have to put up or live with, and there most certainly are things you can do to alleviate them and in turn live a calmer and more fulfilling life.

As with any form of personal development, the key is to identify and understand what is going on for you personally and take small steps forward. If you have experienced stress and anxiety all your life, your brain will likely be quite used to this way of being and will try to 'keep you safe' by keeping things the same. The thing is, without change there is no growth or progress, so please be kind and gentle with yourself and seek professional support if you feel that the trauma that has caused your anxiety and stress is too triggering and is holding you back.

What is anxiety?

Anxiety is a natural response to threat, fear and even pressure that can affect how we think, feel and behave.

What is stress?

Similar to anxiety, stress is the body's reaction to experiencing threat or pressure. A small amount is OK and needed when a genuine threat is present or a deadline is looming; however, when stress becomes long-term or chronic, it can lead to physical and mental health problems and burnout.

Signs of anxiety and stress

Many people who have grown up not knowing they are autistic don't know that they are anxious or stressed, and when they find out what they are, they are often amazed because they thought that this was how 'everyone' experienced the world around them.

Hannah demonstrated this point in her interview:

> Both of my parents are very anxious, so I think there was a time in my life when if someone had said to me, 'Are you anxious?' [I'd say] 'Oh no, no, absolutely not', but looking back, I was incredibly anxious! Because the model of my life has been anxiety, I think I've had an anxiety disorder all my life. There isn't a baseline to go back to and say, this is, you know, normal, calm, because that had never ever been there.

Nikki's health suffered due to the stress of growing up without knowing she was neurodivergent. She said, 'If I was sleeping two hours a night, I'd be amazed. I had chronic insomnia. My health was horrendous, and my brain was wired to the point that I genuinely don't know how I coped.' It's important to remember that anxiety and stress can be very different in different people, and no two people's experiences will be the same.

Here are some signs of anxiety:

- concentration issues
- feeling restless
- feeling worried
- avoiding people/places/situations
- sleep issues
- changes in appetite
- fast heartbeat
- feelings in stomach, such as churning
- increase in repetitive or compulsive thoughts/behaviour
- sweating/hot flushes
- panic attacks
- stimming.

Why are autistic people vulnerable to stress and anxiety?

Due to the unpredictability of the world and the people in it, autistic folk can develop anxiety as the brain's way of trying to protect us from danger. It will try to predict outcomes and seek safety in doing so. This way of being can be extremely tricky and often distressing because we can never know (or control) what others will say or do, and life constantly changes and gets in the way of any plans we make. This conflict creates an ideal situation for anxiety to manifest, and unless it is identified and managed, this anxiety can lead to a vast amount of suffering, confusion, frustration and sorrow.

Many non-identified autistic folk are diagnosed with general anxiety disorder (GAD) before autism is considered, often years later on. Nikki talked about this: 'When I was 18, I was diagnosed with general anxiety disorder, and I'd have full-on panic attacks.

I've had ambulances called because of the extent of my panic attacks over the years.'

Factors affecting stress and anxiety in autistic folks and the effects on everyday living

Environment

Whether we are at home, work or out in public, the environment has the ability to cause stress and anxiety. It is a good idea to know what factors/situations cause stress so that we can take measures to help ourselves and ask for help if needed.

Sensory issues

As discussed in the chapter on sensory processing, there are many sensory triggers that can cause stress and anxiety daily if not addressed and modified.

Needs not being met in the workplace

Nikki talked of working for many years in a role that was misaligned for her on many levels:

> Anxiety and stress were immense for me. The height of my challenges was when I was [working] in corporate, which was as far misaligned for my needs as I could possibly tell you. Travelling two hours a day, being in the HQ environment with toxic people in a toxic company.

It got so bad that at age 36 she drove home one day and thought, 'Drive your car off the road right now, and you won't have to do this anymore. I wasn't going to do it, but the very fact that the thought came into my head meant that this was serious.'

This demonstrates the importance of knowing your needs, your values and your limitations when choosing where you work and the type of work you do.

Often, people tell me they don't know what job they would like to do, and then it is a case of identifying individual needs, wants and interests and researching jobs and employers that will meet requirements. This is easier said than done, of course, but it is a starting point. Also, the idea of self-employment is often a solution for autistic/neurodivergent folk.

Social situations

The unpredictability of conversations can cause a great deal of anxiety in autistic people. This is exacerbated by thoughts of self-doubt ('What if I say the wrong thing?' or 'What if they think I'm weird?'). It is not surprising that we can think like this. So many times, autistic people are ridiculed, bullied and made to feel inferior due to misunderstandings or by 'saying something inappropriate'.

These experiences often start from an early age, as described by Lauren:

> From what I can remember, I used to have a stomach-ache and feel sick on the drive into school [and when attending birthday parties]. I used to worry about what I was going to say to people. If we went on school trips on a bus, I would think, 'Who am I going to sit next to? What are we going to talk about?'

I personally still, as a 48-year-old, have the same worry of 'Who will I sit with?' when attending events and gatherings! The difference now is that I have worked hard on changing my inner dialogue and if the thought pops into my head, I can reassure myself and say/think something like 'You're OK and wherever you sit will be OK. You've got this.'

I know that it is all right to have these worries and that 'I will be OK'. I am comfortable being me. This works 90 per cent of the time, which is great; however, the fear of being left out/excluded does still arise every so often and I know this is something I am still working on, which is OK.

New experiences/environments/people

The autistic brain likes and thrives on predictability (unless combined with an ADHD brain that thrives on change and novelty, like mine and Kate's!). This is a reason why structures and routines are created and followed so that a sense of familiarity and safety is found.

New experiences, places and people are far from familiar and that is why they can be anxiety inducing. This does not mean that us autistic folk should not experience these things, but by understanding where the anxiety/stress is coming from, we are better equipped to manage it and, in many instances, overcome it.

Unpredictability

If there is one thing that is predictable, it is that life is inevitably unpredictable! Many autistic folk attempt to compensate for this by controlling their environment, what happens, what they will say and so on. This is all very well and can create a sense of calm and safety – until something or someone does not go according to plan! We simply cannot control what others do, say or think. We are only in control of ourselves, our ideas and our actions.

Not knowing

I don't know about you, but I have spent much of my life stressing over not knowing. In particular, it's not knowing what others are thinking and how they are feeling, especially if they leave an argument/disagreement halfway through (for whatever reason) and refuse to communicate and let me know where I stand and what is happening. Or situations like not knowing why my manager has called an unplanned meeting with me without any explanation. The list is endless, and I know that this causes so much unease, stress and anxiety for many of us.

Perfectionism

Alice stated:

> A lot of my anxiety is about getting things wrong, people not liking me, always feeling a bit 'less than' and disappointed in myself, like I haven't really achieved the things I ought to have achieved. [That] I don't have the life I feel that I should have had.

Many autistic people I have met – both children and adults – have perfectionist traits. I describe myself as a 'recovering perfectionist', which is a very freeing position to be in. Ten years ago, I would have really struggled to write this book due to worries around if it would be good enough, what people would think and who am I to be writing such a book.

I would have been paralyzed with fear about doing things wrong, which meant I became an expert at avoiding situations that would involve receiving feedback in case there was 'room for improvement'. Goodness me, when I think about how life was, I realize how exhausting it was!

Change (however big or small, including unexpected changes)

Change is inevitable and part of life. It can be the cause of so much anxiety and stress, especially when we don't know that change is causing us issues or it is 'forced' on us at short notice and without explanation. The impact of change should not be underestimated, and it may be helpful to remember that with any change comes loss and from loss comes grief. It is also worth highlighting that all feelings are valid, and however you feel about a change, no matter how big or seemingly small, it is your experience, which cannot be taken away from you.

Other sources of stress and anxiety

Other sources of stress and anxiety include, but are not limited to:

- not feeling listened to/heard/respected

- being and feeling misunderstood
- difficulties with emotions
- masking
- tiredness
- overwhelm
- over- and under-stimulation
- communication needs.

Looking at some of the factors that affect stress and anxiety and the complex ways they can manifest and intertwine with being autistic, it is not surprising that many autistic folk are chronically stressed and anxious.

But it's not all doom and gloom, because once we know what is happening and why, we can do something about it.

Our interviewees provided lots of useful tips and strategies that can be used straight away. My one piece of advice around this is to choose one tip at a time and implement it slowly and with self-compassion. Be mindful that new ways of being take time, practice and intention. And remember, even though you are trying to improve things for yourself, your brain may resist at first because, well, it's change! Even good change can be difficult, and the brain will need time to process and catch up with where you want to be!

What helps reduce stress and anxiety?
Creating safety

The anxious brain doesn't feel safe, so creating feelings of safety can help reduce the anxiety. Many autistic folks talk of watching the same films/TV shows repeatedly as it helps soothe their systems, is predictable and feels safe. According to Hannah:

> The little things that make you feel safe are the same: the same food, the same blanket, the same TV show or the same book that I can go into and I know what's going to happen and I know the

people in the story and I know they're going to be kind. I read and watch things about kind people so I can go into that world that isn't mine, that I have no part of, and feel safe in there.

Spending time on passions and interests

This is often a go-to for anxious autistic folk. Jeff explained:

> Two of my passions are playing the piano and playing tennis. Both help me deal with stress and anxiety. I work from home, and sometimes will take a short break to go play the piano for a while. It is a safe way for me to express myself through music.

Routines

Routines and rituals can help reduce anxiety and help with predictability. According to Jeff:

> Some autistic people are drawn towards animals and I definitely fall into that camp. I love cats. It is a running joke in the community that cats are quite similar to autistic people, in that they can be very independent and love their routines. My two cats and I work together like clockwork, performing our routines every day at the exact same times. They really help me to stay regulated and ease some of my anxiety.

Visual schedules

Having visual aids can be transformational and can help with memory issues as well as decision making as the decisions are made in advance (there is more about this in Chapter 4: Executive Functioning). Ruth said that 'using a whiteboard or days of the week whiteboard to write down what's happening and when' is helpful for reducing anxiety and promoting calm.

Communicating one's own needs

Ruth explained: 'When it comes to noise, I let people know that

I find that difficult (if I feel able to disclose) and they might feel more able to tell me when noise might be happening so I can go out or I know when to expect it.'

Taking control

Lyn talked about how she manages anxiety by being in control. She does this by being organized and gathering facts about different situations. For example, if one of her children is going on a school trip, she will ensure that she knows exactly what they need to take. Taking control and knowing all the facts about things that are causing her anxiety has helped her to manage it. The downside can be that she might be a bit rigid in how she feels things need to be done, and others may not be on board with her ideas.

Getting comfortable with discomfort

This has been life-changing for me. By accepting that many things will bring feelings of discomfort and my traditional approach of avoiding people, places and situations was no longer serving me, I recognized that I had to find a way to navigate this while honouring my needs.

Around 13 years ago, I discovered comedy improvisation, and I can honestly say it has changed my life. To learn how to create short scenes in the moment where you can pretty much say what you like (within reason) without fear of persecution for saying the 'wrong' thing is such a freeing process and experience.

To do improvisation, you have to listen to what is said to you in the moment and respond only to that, so there is no planning in advance what to say, no pressure to 'get it right'. If you follow the rules by listening and responding to what you hear, you cannot get it wrong.

Improvisation for me has been transformational, and as an autistic ADHDer, it works so well for my brain as there are clear rules and structures as well as freedom to do, say and create whatever my brain thinks of.

It is pure joy and has helped my anxiety in so many ways. Even the act of improvising is a form of meditation because the brain is so engaged in the scene that I don't think of anything else. As with any skill, it takes time, practice and commitment, but the payoff is priceless. Oh, and it's so much fun!

I understand that improvisation may not be for everyone, but it demonstrates that with the right intentions/goals, support and determination, it is possible to get comfortable with discomfort. The key, as always, is to start small and recognize the small wins along the way.

Boundaries

Setting boundaries to protect ourselves is essential for managing stress and anxiety. See Chapter 5: Communication, and Chapter 16: Getting to Know Yourself for more on this.

Being true to yourself

Being authentic and proud is something that has helped me so much over the years. Since realizing I was neurodivergent about 16 years ago, I have spent a great deal of time finding out about who I really am and uncovering the parts of me that I had hidden away. I believe the path to being my true self is one that will continue throughout my lifetime, and although there is sadness and a lot of 'what ifs' to grieve for and heal through, it also feels hugely exciting and full of possibilities.

Self-compassion/self-coaching

When we learn to be curious and ask ourselves questions, we can open ourselves up to new ways of thinking as well as new possibilities. Nikki suggested:

> Think about how you are feeling and what you need in that moment. Do you need to not do the thing? Do you need to mask and camouflage to get through? Do you need some support? Being able

to ask and advocate for yourself, for what you need, can be so helpful.

Mindfulness

This can take many forms and it's well worth experimenting with to find what works for you. Nikki said:

> The advice that I give to people who are telling me that they're stressed is to listen for the sound of the birds singing as the birds only sing when it's safe. So, if I feel stressed and anxious, I try to find a park or somewhere where there's some wildlife; if I can hear the birds singing, it's reassuring to me.

She also shared, 'If I'm feeling anxious and stressed, I imagine that those stressful moments and thoughts and feelings are clouds in the sky and they're just going to drift on over. They're just going to float on by, and they'll be gone.'

Breath work has been helpful for me for reducing stress and anxiety both in the moment and through daily practice (almost daily – still a work in progress). Done in the right way, breath work can regulate the nervous system within minutes, reduce blood pressure and bring about feelings of calm and clarity. Again, it's well worth experimenting with what works for you. There are plenty of videos on YouTube and recordings on Spotify, as well as in-person classes.

Another tool I use for managing stress, energy, tiredness and general wellbeing is yoga nidra, which is deep, relaxing guided meditation, done while lying down. The exercises can be found on YouTube and via app stores. Because they are guided, I find them easier to follow, even with my 'busy brain'.

KATE'S TOP ANXIETY BUSTERS

In addition to all of Suzi's excellent suggestions, I want to share three things that have helped me enormously over the past few years.

'Will it matter in a year?'
When something stressful happens, I ask myself, 'Will it matter in a year?' Ninety-nine per cent of the time, it won't. We can create huge anxiety over things like accidentally cutting someone off in traffic or making a mistake at work. In a year, you will probably have forgotten all about it.

'That is not happening now'
I sometimes find myself caught up in a doom spiral about something that may or may not happen in the future. I find it helpful to remind myself that whatever it is I am worried about is not happening right now. This helps me to be present in the moment and let whatever is going to happen, happen.

'Whatever's gonna happen...'
Writing that last tip reminded me of some great advice a friend gave me last year. I was stressed about an upcoming hospital visit for my daughter. He said, 'Don't stress about it; whatever's gonna happen is gonna happen.' He was right. The hospital visit was successful and I've used that advice many times since then.

Exercise
Exercise is a known stress buster and has so many benefits. Finding the right way to exercise and move is the trickier part and is the key to building it into our lives. When deciding on exercise or movement, it might be helpful to consider the following:

- What are your reasons for wanting to exercise?
- What difference will it make to your life?

- What do you truly enjoy doing?
- What did you enjoy in the past that you could try again?
- What do you need to know before joining a class/gym/group and so on?
- Do you prefer to exercise alone or with someone else?
- What sensory needs do you have to consider?
- What is stopping you from going ahead?
- What do you need to go ahead and start exercising?
- What are the firsts steps you need to take to move forward with your exercise goals?

Bear in mind that exercise doesn't have to be a big, formal thing. It can just be five minutes here and there of bouncing on an exercise ball or using resistance bands. Anything that uses big muscles in your body will help to reduce anxiety.

Journalling

Journalling can help immensely with all of the thoughts and feelings that we can hold in on a daily basis. When we don't express ourselves, our bodies hold on to the stress and can make us ill, irritable and, well, stressed! Writing down our thoughts and feelings can be healing and cathartic, and can help us make sense of who we are.

There is no need to buy a fancy journal unless you want to. Any notebook will work or even the notes app on a phone or indeed a laptop – whatever works for you!

Here are a few prompts to get you started:

- List three strengths or skills.
- What makes you happy?
- What makes you sad?
- What are your hopes for the day?
- Think about a time when you overcame a challenge. What skills or strengths did you use? How did it make you feel?

- Write about someone you feel grateful for.

Kate journals every day and shares more about this in Chapter 7: Emotions. She says, 'Writing helps me work through whatever is on my mind. Often, it's like having a conversation with myself and it allows me to solve problems in a clear and pragmatic way.'

As with all of the tips, information and guidance in this book, it is important to do what works for you. No two people in the world are the same and therefore they need different things. Part of the journey of self-discovery is experimenting and finding out what works for us and our unique brains.

Please remember that stress is not something we have to 'put up with' and that we can control what we do about it. With the right support and tools, life does not have to be so stressful.

— Chapter 10 —

Pathological Demand Avoidance (PDA)

SUZI

In this chapter, I discuss pathological demand avoidance (PDA) as it resonates with me. Although widely understood to be a profile of autism, it is not currently an official diagnosis, so that is why we decided to include it here rather than in the co-occurring conditions chapter.

According to the PDA Society in the UK, PDA is generally understood to be a profile on the autism spectrum, involving the avoidance of everyday demands and the use of 'social' strategies as part of this avoidance.

Autistic people with a PDA profile often:

- 'have a need for control which is often anxiety related
- are driven to avoid everyday demands and expectations (including things that they want to do or enjoy) to an extreme extent
- tend to use approaches that are 'social in nature' in order to avoid demands
- present with many of the 'key features' of PDA rather than just one or two
- tend not to respond to conventional parenting, teaching or support approaches.'[1]

The concept of demands has taken me a long time to grasp because they can be literally everyday things such as rules, instructions, requests, promises (I try not to make them, because as soon as I do, I feel anxious and pressured to follow through), expectations and even visual signs like 'Keep off the grass', to which my automatic response is 'You keep off the grass, you can't tell me what to do!'

When thinking about PDA, it is really important to recognize that avoiding demands is a case of 'can't, not won't', and even though that is tricky to comprehend, it is helpful to refer to when you are struggling to do something 'easy' or 'pleasurable' and to realize you are not 'bad', 'lazy' or unmotivated; you are stuck.

Kyra talked about when she first began to understand she could have PDA. She had realized that she might be autistic, but in reading the experiences of other autistic people, there were similarities, but she still felt 'different'. When she discovered her PDA, she said:

> It was a huge epiphany moment. Not only did this describe my eldest but also myself! I had spent years, most of my life up until that point, feeling broken, defective, that I had failed, and despite all my efforts to be 'better', I just couldn't do what others seemed to find so easy.

The more I am learning about PDA, the more it makes sense to me and I really feel that it is a big piece of the picture for me. It explains so much, and with this awareness, I am able to better understand my needs and advocate for myself and others.

Let's now look at some ways in which PDA shows up for me and Kyra, as well as some strategies to help.

Praise and how it can make me feel

This is a complex one because growing up as a people pleaser, I was often dependent on praise to know that I was OK, that I was enough.

Praise is such a subjective concept, and for me as a PDAer, I have realized that in certain contexts it can really trigger me. A coach I once worked with expressed how much she loved working with other coaches and that I was doing so well. For context, I was 'doing well' at that point in time – the subject was new and therefore exciting and interesting.

The moment she said that, I felt the pressure of expectation hit me straight away. 'Oh great, now I have to carry on "doing so well".' Then the resentment came: 'She doesn't even know me, how can she make such a bold judgement? Just because I am a coach does not mean I don't have struggles and challenges.' The thoughts spiralled so quickly it was hard to stop them. 'I am doing well but I know at some point I will struggle, and now I don't feel as if I can tell her when I do because she now has a big expectation of me.'

Did the coach do anything wrong? Not really. She intended to be encouraging, but in those short comments she made it about her ('I love working with other coaches') which I now know was not a reflection on me; however, in that moment, I was triggered. This is a really good insight into how praise can backfire, even when the intentions of the praise giver are good. How did I manage the situation? In the moment, I said nothing, and later I reflected on my response and how what she said was about her and not me. This helped me feel better about the situation and for me was another self-awareness moment.

I also ruminated for a few days and then discussed it with my other coach of two years, with whom I share a lot (unmasked, thank goodness). We discussed how people are not always aware of the impact of their words on others, and for a non-PDAer, those words may have had a positive impact. I did not share how I felt with the coach who said it, mainly because I did not have the energy or even the language to explain.

Self-advocacy can take a lot of effort, and we have to choose when to speak up and when to speak to someone we trust. These days, I am more able to recognize that praise/feedback can be used as evidence for what I already know and that I don't have to have a big emotional attachment to what is said.

Completing tasks while people are watching

Argh! I was always so confused as to why I had such an issue with this. My earlier memories are from school when the teacher would 'lurk' behind me while I was trying to work. I could sense their creepy presence behind me, and I would freeze, unable to think or do. It was horrible, confusing and rather irritating. As a teacher, I was very conscious not to do this to my students.

As an adult, I hate being watched while doing everyday activities like cooking, opening the front door with a key and even finding a film or TV show via the TV remote. Last night I was searching for a programme and having some difficulty, and I said to my wife, 'I know where it is, don't say anything', to which she replied, 'I wasn't going to', and we both laughed. I feel a sense of panic if I think someone is going to tell me how to do something I am doing or about to do!

Identifying emotions

I am extremely comfortable in character role play and improvisation and admit that I have been known to use charm and words to get what I want/my own way. I didn't realize this was what I was doing as I didn't have the awareness, and now that I do, I am very mindful of how I react and respond when things don't go my way. I am more open to acknowledging and sitting with my emotions, especially tricky ones, and am able to soothe myself by saying/thinking to myself, 'You're OK, you are safe' or 'I am experiencing frustration; this is OK, it will pass.'

When we identify and acknowledge our feelings and emotions, we are more equipped to let them 'ride the wave', and eventually they dissipate and release. It's when we try to ignore them or push them down that they get stuck and can cause unhappiness and rumination. When we ignore the underlying emotions, our thoughts can get stuck in a loop saying things like, 'I didn't even ask for her opinion, why did she give it?' over and over again, which is infuriating to say the least.

One book that has really helped me to identify and understand a variety of emotions is *Atlas of the Heart* by Brené Brown.[2] Brené is an 'emotions researcher' and breaks down a range of emotions (positive and difficult), explaining what can cause them and how to process and manage them. It's brilliant (in my opinion) and such a useful resource, especially for us autistic folks who can have difficulty identifying and understanding how we feel. I have also found it helpful for understanding the emotions and behaviours of others, which in turn has helped me realize that what anyone else says or does is about them, not me. This is a great antidote to rejection sensitivity dysphoria, which is discussed in more detail in the next chapter.

Can't, not won't

I find being PDA quite confusing, as I often find that I genuinely can't do things I really want to do, such as go for a swim, walk, work out or even write this book. It's been hard to get my head around the fact that it's actually a can't rather than a won't, and I'm still working through that one.

PDAers are said to be comfortable with role play and often with being in charge. When I am in charge or have a specific role, it helps me feel grounded and in control. When I don't have a role, I feel lost and left out and as if I'm drifting around in limbo.

Kyra talked about a job she had as a bar manager which she 'thoroughly enjoyed', where she was often able to work through her day with little direction and thus her autonomy felt satisfied – the mix of spontaneity and personal responsibility sat well with her.

When I think back to my days of being employed by someone, I realize now why I had such issues with my line managers, especially the ones who tried to get involved too heavily in my work! As soon as a manager started micromanaging me, it was never long before I resigned and got a new job.

Kyra talked of similar experiences:

> I needed to feel respected and valued, but at the same time also trusted to be able to meet the role without 'micromanagement' or a heavy-handed approach. As soon as a role became 'demanding', then I would start to dip sharply in my ability and quality of engagement, and this was often hard as it could be seen as being unreliable or not being a good fit for the role – but this was never for a lack of trying!

For me, PDA shows up in many ways which are often subtle and invisible to the onlooker. For example, I can't do something if I'm told or even advised to. I won't necessarily say no or kick up a fuss; it's more of a subtle avoidance – it feels like a reflex and feels wrong.

So, never tell me I 'should' do something (or expect me to do something) because it's likely to never happen, regardless of how positive the outcome. I feel very pressured by any whiff of expectation.

I got really annoyed once when I was at the cinema with a good friend who kept laughing at the film, then looking at me to see if I was laughing, too. I was not, and the more she looked at me, the more pressure I felt, and the more upset and annoyed I became. Basically, my highly sensitive nervous system sees demands, requests and expectations as a threat to my autonomy.

What helps?
Autonomy
When asked what helps, Kyra said, 'I need a certain amount of autonomy like others need air. This means being able to dictate my

own actions and follow my own spontaneity.' She continued, 'I find trying to have a fairly low arousal environment and the ability to try to explain to others as to why I cannot do something and that that is respected and understood help hugely.' This really demonstrates the need to have supportive people around you as well as the confidence and language to let others know what you need.

'I get to do...'

In my experience of PDA, it can be quite a challenge to get my brain to cooperate and I often find ways to trick it. Take my 'to do' list, for example. I do not ever call it a 'to do list'. Instead, I call it a 'get to do list'. This subtle change of wording has made a big difference to how I approach tasks that, let's face it, have to be done. If they make it on to the list, they are highly important to me. By thinking about them as things I 'get to do', I am in a grateful frame of mind and I think of how much I love working for myself, and yes, although they are not always exciting, I am privileged to be in a position where I 'get to do' the stuff that makes my business or personal life happy.

Kyra spoke of her own internal game, which she jokingly called 'PDA Top Trumps'. In this game, there will be tasks that need to be done, and some are more important than others. 'Some tasks can be completed at the expense of "avoiding" others. This can be a game of risk at times, but also often the only way that at least some of the things get done, if not all of them!'

Asking for help and trusting others

I am fiercely independent, and sometimes this is to my detriment, as asking for support and help can be difficult. I am learning that it's OK to ask for help, and that trusting others (the right ones) is a good thing.

This takes time, awareness, patience and self-compassion and acceptance of what the reality is.

We cannot understand ourselves if we aren't aware of our

unique way of being, what we need and the way our brains work. We can find ways to help ourselves do something that make it feel like our own idea or decision.

Reframing the demand

Time is often helpful. If I let some time pass, then the intensity of the demand is less or even gone. Reframing and self-talk are critical to moving forward – for example, reframing 'I'm not doing what they tell me to do' to 'I am in control of what I do or don't do'.

'I have a choice always' or 'I can/will do it in my own time' can help you to get unstuck. Not always, of course. But the more often you find reframes that work for you, the more your brain will get used to them and will start to respond in a way that serves you.

I won't tell you to try it as that may feel 'demandy'. But what I will say is that it's your choice, and if you want to experiment with these strategies, then you can if you want. If you don't, then don't.

Kyra commented, 'PDA may be complex but so is life, and both are beautiful for their challenges, experiences and the lessons we learn on the way. Dance through the chaos, laugh with the storm and bask in sunshine.'

And her last piece of advice, should you wish to take it or not (up to you, of course), was 'You've got this – and when you don't, there are others out there holding the space for you until you can return, bigger and better than before.'

So, does PDA resonate with you? Are you surprised by any of the insights? It is worth remembering that although PDA is a profile of autism it won't apply to every autistic person and that is OK. What is most important is the individual journey of learning and self-discovery.

— Chapter 11 —

Rejection Sensitivity Dysphoria (RSD)

SUZI

Rejection sensitivity dysphoria (RSD) is not a diagnosable condition, but rather a common manifestation of years of negative messaging received by many neurodivergent folks. For this reason, it does not appear in the co-occurring conditions section.

RSD is an extreme, emotionally painful reaction to criticism and/or rejection and is often associated with ADHD, although many autistic folks talk of experiencing it, too. In this chapter, I will explore what RSD is and some of the different ways it can manifest and show up. I'll also provide some strategies, tips and techniques to start to overcome this painful part of being neurodivergent, which can impact every area of life.

If you have been told you are too much, too sensitive, too intense or anything else that feels like an attack on the essence of who you are, then you may also experience RSD. Neurodivergent folks receive thousands of negative messages throughout their lifetime, which can cause low self-esteem and confidence and, not surprisingly, manifest in experiencing RSD.

Being autistic and having a literal understanding of language, I used to think that other people's opinions were the truth. I honestly didn't know that opinions were just that and not the truth. They are certainly not my truth!

For me, this is one of the reasons I developed perfectionism and how RSD became such a feature of my life. I took what others said as my truth and learned to set myself unrealistic standards that were extremely hard to meet, so that I could live up to what I thought others expected of me. It was exhausting, and I lost myself!

Now I know what was happening and I am more aware of myself, I am putting a stop to it and – guess what? – it feels amazing! I feel free. What about you? Are you breaking free from other people's expectations?

As an autistic person, I often don't pick up on certain cues or intent unless the other person states very clearly and directly what they mean.

During an event I held called ADHD The Experience, I thought I was being heckled during my talk about, ironically 'kicking RSD's butt', but, apparently, I was being complimented! I'm still not sure how, but as an experienced improviser and speaker, I think I handled it very well. I haven't always handled it well, though, and for many years (my whole life up until about five years ago) I spiralled into negative thought patterns (and therefore RSD) whenever I was unsure of or misunderstood the intentions of others. It did not occur to me that not everything that was said to me was personal.

Around five years ago, when I was working for a charity, I attended a training event (on mental health) and the trainer told us all to get into groups of five. I did not know anyone there and I was left standing in the middle of the room waiting for a group to call me over. I felt so alone, my heart hurt, and I could feel the tears building in my eyes. I wanted to leave, and it took all my strength to stay and approach an established group and suggest I join them. It took about an hour to recover from this perceived rejection, and it impacted how I interacted for the rest of the day. Nobody in that session realized how I felt. How could they? I masked my way through it and pretended all was well.

The reality was that no one had set out to reject me. People can be like sheep and flock in a panic to the nearest group without a thought for those who may be left out. I very much doubt that there was any ill intent from anyone that day. I don't understand this mentality myself, probably due to years of it happening to me, so I am extra vigilant of others who may be feeling left out, and I make sure I include them.

How to recover from RSD

One way to recover from RSD is to discover who you really are under the mask and break free from social conditioning that tells us we should be a certain way and be able to do all the things, and that basically we are not good enough – none of which is true.

You need to find out what your core beliefs are, because if they include 'I am not good enough', then RSD is always going to rear its head! This is by no means easy work, and you might need support to work through it from a therapist, coach or even self-help books. It is essential that we work with our core beliefs and in time replace them with new beliefs that serve us well and empower us.

When you feel criticized or rejected, it can help to stop, pause and remember that we are GOOD people with good intentions. Remember that whatever anyone says or thinks about you is NOT about you. It is about them, their story and the unique lens through which they are viewing you. When we accept the opinions of others as our truth, we lose our power! We literally give our power to someone else.

Awareness is the key here, and it's important to get to know what your triggers are for feeling rejected or criticized. Then work to identify the automatic thoughts such as 'Why don't they like me?', 'They think I'm weird/intense' or 'My work is never good enough', as these thoughts are what create the feelings of shame, frustration, guilt and so on, which can be so painful to experience.

One way we try to avoid these painful feelings is to aim to do everything perfectly and therefore avoid the criticism of others. The main flaws here, though, are that there is no such thing as 'perfect' and we cannot control what others say, think or do, so avoidance is not a sustainable (or healthy) coping mechanism.

The ultimate outcome would be to rewire the brain's neural pathways with kinder, more compassionate thoughts such as 'I am OK', 'I am a good/caring/kind person', 'I have done nothing wrong' and 'I am doing my best and that is good enough'.

When we can focus on thinking differently (this takes time, effort, practice and patience), we can literally create new pathways and therefore beliefs within the brain that eventually will become the louder, more automatic thoughts which in turn make for more pleasurable feelings.

As I said, this all takes time and effort and often needs the help of a professional such as a therapist, counsellor or coach. This is confronting work and it's important to feel ready to address it and to feel supported while you do. I am quite far along in my journey of overcoming RSD, and I still get upset when I revisit the sad and difficult memories that have ultimately shaped my life and who I am. As with everything, please practise self-compassion as that is where your power lies and where change is possible.

What else helps? Tips for helping with RSD
Find space
When you feel your body 'flooding' with emotion, say: 'Excuse me, I don't feel good. I need to leave.'

Breath work
Breathe in through your nose while expanding your stomach and chest then breathe out through your nose. Do this up to ten times (or more if you want to). This will give your body and brain time to overcome the rush of adrenaline and cortisol, and help you think more clearly.

Express your emotions
Find ways of getting emotions out of your system that work for you such as drawing, colouring or painting. Talk to someone you trust

about how you are feeling. Go for a walk or run, go to the gym, do some dancing. Write or journal – try putting names to the emotions you feel.

Distract yourself

Play a game on your phone or computer, play with a pet, watch a TV show or film, look at photos, do something that brings you joy and comfort.

Talk about and express your needs

Ask for what you need: 'I appreciate your feedback. I am sensitive, so please can you tell me what I am doing well and then how I can improve.'

Get advance warning

To prevent worrying about what someone might want to talk to you about, say to them, 'Please can you let me know what you want to talk about? It really helps me to know so that I don't worry.' Remember that what other people say about you is about them and not you. It is about their life lens, their experiences and their feelings. If someone gives you their opinion, it is just that – their opinion. Remember: opinions are not facts!

Do more of what you are good at

Love art? Do more. Love sport? Join that club you have been thinking about. Love performing? Join that acting class. Love to write? Write. Need novelty and new things in your life? See what's on in your local area.

Practise thinking (while creating new pathways that serve) intentional thoughts

Some examples of intentional thoughts are:

- I am a kind and capable person.

- I am enough.
- I am doing my best right now.
- I am OK.
- I can cope.
- I am highly sensitive and that is OK.

Growing up with unidentified ADHD, autism, Tourette's and OCD left me feeling 'stupid' and different for most of my life. How could I be so good at some things like sports and writing yet so terrible at maths and science? I believed there was 'something wrong with me'.

The result of this kind of thinking was seriously low self-esteem, self-worth and confidence, and a huge helping of RSD! The self-doubt and lack of trust all shaped my experience of the world and my sense of self.

I am happy to say that 11 years post diagnosis I am literally thriving and using my unique brain's strengths, my journey and my experiences to live the life I love and deserve.

There was never anything wrong with me and there is nothing wrong with you, my neurodivergent friend. With the right support to heal and grow and create an environment where we can flourish, we can live a life of joy and passion.

Part 3

DEALING WITH OTHER PEOPLE

— Chapter 12 —

Disclosure

KATE

On a weekly basis, newspaper headlines and social media stories herald the message that autism is bad. We are told that autistic people do bad things, autistic people are unable to live fulfilling lives, and autistic people are somehow defective.

On the other hand, autism is everywhere in popular culture. *A Kind of Spark*, *Heartbreak High*, *Dinosaur* and *Extraordinary Attorney Woo* are just a few of many TV shows and films featuring autistic characters enjoying various life successes. For the average person, the message about autism is confusing: autistic people do bad things (think the Sandy Hook shooter,* and so on**), but they can also be quirky, cute and have genius superpowers.

Disclosure as a public service

The general public seems to hold the deeply entrenched idea that

---

* A mass shooting occurred in December 2012 in an elementary school in Newtown, Connecticut, where 26 people were shot and killed, most of them children. It was later reported that the 20-year-old shooter, Adam Lanza, had Asperger's syndrome.

** To be clear, I am not saying I feel the negative actions of these individuals is due to them being autistic. I am simply pointing out that the media make these kinds of negative connections on a daily basis.

'autism' and 'capable' are mutually exclusive. The view seems to be that although there are successful autistic characters on television, these are not real people, nor do they represent real people in the real world.

Some of our interviewees are both autistic and have ADHD. There is a clear divide between how people in general view autism and ADHD. Most of society confuses autism with severe learning disability, and so discounts the capability and competency of autistic people as a whole. On the flipside, ADHD seems to have a cache of 'cool'. The general consensus seems to be that ADHD people are arty, quirky, creative and think outside the box. Interviewees who are both autistic and have ADHD reported feeling perfectly comfortable disclosing their ADHD while being very closed off when it came to talking about autism. This has certainly been the case for me.

When I discovered that I am autistic in 2013, I was a few years into running an organization supporting parents of autistic children. I had a small team that I had recruited (many of whom were also parents of autistic children). It felt important to tell them about being autistic, and I did so, expecting support and understanding. What actually happened was that some of them did not believe me. To these individuals, I was not like their own experiences of autism, and so could not be autistic. However, despite their disbelief, they began to treat me differently. They would speak to me as though everything needed very careful explanation. I was made to feel that maybe I could not do the job I had been doing very successfully, for the organization I had founded myself.

This experience sent me underground with my autism. In fact, over a decade later, I am still a bit scarred by this and am extremely selective about who I disclose to. This sort of experience happened to Nick as well. He was waiting in a burger van queue at a music festival, and happened to be wearing a badge that said 'I'm not rude, I'm autistic'. When he got to the front of the queue, he got chatting with the woman serving customers. After a few minutes of 'normal' conversation, she clocked the badge and said to him, in a voice you might use with a toddler, 'Oh, that's a nice water bottle you've got there.' It's as though being autistic somehow infantalizes us.

When I went for my autism assessment, I couldn't bear the idea of asking my family to complete the paperwork to support my belief that I am autistic.* I knew that they would not be able to even consider this possibility. Sure enough, a few years ago I won a big award for the work I do in supporting parents of autistic children. When I told family members, some of them disputed the fact that the article described me as autistic. I didn't try to discuss it again

Disclosing our autism can be a way of creating normalcy around it. Bridget spoke of how disclosing to the people around us might create a ripple effect. She pointed out that the more of us who talk about being autistic – the more colourful the mosaic, the more vibrant the picture – the clearer we make it to the world that autism is a rich and varied thing.

Rico said this best:

> My boss at the moment, she knows I'm ADHD, but when I disclosed the autism, she said to me, 'Oh wow, you're very high functioning.' I thought, 'OK, is that supposed to be a compliment? It's kind of a little bit offensive. So [it's like this boss is saying] 'Autistic people are just going to be waste of time, but you happen not to be, so you must be the exception in autistic people.' And for that I would like to raise my voice when I need to raise my voice, and if I can do something about it, I will, as I feel quite passionate about fighting injustice.

Hello world! I'm autistic!

Many of us, when we first realize we are autistic, want to shout it

---

* Inexplicably, however, when I went for assessment for ADHD, I felt comfortable asking for help from my family. It's sad how autism is viewed so differently.

from the rooftops. We can have a naivety about how the people around us will respond to this news. Understanding that we are autistic explains why life has been so very difficult and why sometimes 'easy' tasks are hard for us. It also helps us to see why relationships with friends, partners and family have been fraught with stress and misunderstandings. We want to tell people we are autistic because we believe that it will explain why we are the way we are.

It's important to be mindful of the fact that disclosing autism is not like a get-out-of-jail-free card. It is a delicate balance between explaining the challenges we face and not using being autistic as an excuse for what others might perceive as bad behaviour.

I find this difficult. Recently, I sent a very carelessly worded email to someone in my field. I said all the wrong things and afterwards I apologized by saying that I am autistic and sometimes I don't communicate well. I felt bad about this as, in reality, I should have taken more care, reread and edited the email before sending it. Sometimes in disclosing in this way, we make things worse. It's as though we are saying, 'We autistics can't be trusted to be careful with other people's feelings.'

Overcoming shame

Often, we have to get over our own shame about being autistic, and shame can be a huge factor in a person's decision on whether or not to disclose. This was a pervasive feeling among our interviewees. For some of us, when we recognize we are autistic, the new lenses we see our lives through shine a hard spotlight on all of the many ways we've cocked things up because we did not understand our neurodivergence. This can be excruciatingly embarrassing. For me, seeing all of the things I did – the masking, the tactless things I said, the places where I got things socially so wrong – was very hard to come to terms with. For some of us, saying 'I am autistic' can feel a little like 'I am autistic (and I'm really, really fucked up)'.

Hannah told me that she had consciously determined 'acceptable' ways of expressing her autisticness. These were mainly ways of stimming that could come across as quirky and/or cute: 'Things have been divided into shameful and non-shameful in my head and [I'm] trying to pick apart the shameful things.'

Sarah shared, 'I feel quite embarrassed. I admit that having these labels attached to me has just... I've had such a resistance to it. You know, the vocabulary around the [autism] stuff is unbelievably unkind.'

Jeff, who was 59 at the time of our interview, admitted that at the time he began to realize he is autistic, his own understanding of autism was deeply misinformed. This has had an impact on his decision to disclose or not to disclose, as he understood that the people he might disclose to may be similarly misinformed. He said:

> At this point in my life I'm focused on making it to the finish line of my career and retiring. I know that I am fortunate to be employed. Many of us are not so lucky. I have been at the same job for many years so I decided to disclose my autism diagnosis at work. However, I am still careful about who I tell, because of the stigma surrounding autism and the misunderstanding.

I think a lot of this is about the language that was used about disability in general when we were children. As I mention elsewhere in this book, my family were very anti anything that was different from what society considered 'normal' (in the 1970s!). Anyone who looked different or acted in a way that was 'weird' was openly criticized. This has had a major impact on me. It wasn't until I began to learn about autism through my daughter's diagnosis (and the medical model of disability that I mention in Chapter 2) that I began to break free from these antiquated ideas. However, the scars from this kind of upbringing are deep and long-lasting.

I love Nick's attitude about this:

> I'm also sort of at the point now where I've started to think, 'Well,

fuck you.' It's not my problem, right? If you want to be offended, that's your choice, right? I'm gonna be me. I don't care what you happen to think about it. If you like me, fantastic. If you don't, I don't care.

As I've got older (especially since turning 50), I have found it easier to embrace this kind of mentality, too.

Rico shared:

> I think all these labels, these diagnostic labels, they don't define me necessarily as in 'I'm ADHD'. That's not the first thing I want to say to anybody. Or 'I'm autistic'. Or 'I'm AuDHD' or whatever. It's the same thing as I don't say 'I'm gay', because I don't think I need to present that [like a] business card. But they are an integral part of my personality and I've come to realize [this] pretty late in life. And actually, I'm really happy that I have, and I think all of that has played a role in me feeling better physically as well.

What will people think?

One of the greatest life lessons I've learned in recent years is that what other people think of me is none of my business. This can be valuable when disclosing, but when the person you are disclosing to is a close friend or relative, the worry about what they think can be huge.

We cannot predict how people will feel when we disclose that we are autistic. Even with people we are close to, we don't know their history with disability or their level of understanding about autism. I am very open about being autistic with the people in my life. Where in the past I have felt shame about social gaffes or relationship disasters (that came about due to masking or other autism-related issues), now I am compassionate with myself about these kinds of things. When I share my autisticness with my friends, it helps them to be compassionate with themselves, too.

How and when you disclose will depend very much on your current life situation. I would advise you to resist the urge to tell everyone all at once. I know you may be excited and wanting to share this huge news, but more careful consideration is needed. Some people just tell immediate family, or just their partner and closest friends.

Talking about her partner, Katharine shared, 'Discovering that I'm autistic has improved our relationship a lot because suddenly he understands finally that there is no hidden context, there's no hidden meaning.'

Lyn told us:

Well, I openly say it with my close family, so my husband and my boys. And I think actually it's helped my husband understand me a lot more because obviously he's learning to understand the [autistic] boys and then you see similar behaviour. So, I think that that's really helped. And then with close family and friends, like my brother and my closest female friends, I've sort of said it in conversation. But I've never directly said it to them.

Some find that drip-feeding information to those around them and not ever actually saying the words 'I'm autistic' works perfectly well. Others feel that being very open about it is better for them. Some people decide not to disclose at all and simply explore their autisticness on their own.

Lauren told me, 'I've not really told anybody, but I know that it wouldn't really make any difference to them because it's just a label and they don't get it. Unless you've kind of been through it, you don't get it.'

Remember that you have likely been thinking about, reading about, watching TikToks about and generally inhaling information about autism for ages. Your friend/mum/lover has not had the benefit of this. So, they will not have the insight you do when you tell them. You'll need to be very patient and compassionate when sharing this news.

The general consensus is that the response to disclosure will go one of two ways. Either the person you disclose to will be entirely incredulous and discount your diagnosis/self-identification or they will say, 'Well, yes I know' (and you may think, 'Well, why didn't you tell *me*?').

It's generally best to let the person you are disclosing to come to terms with the information in their own way. It's tempting to give our friend, parent or partner a stack of books and a list of YouTube links in the hope that they will consume it all and become an enlightened being. However, it is often far more helpful to be the gentle educator. Make it clear to the person you are speaking to that you are open to any questions they have. Be patient with the people you tell; they will need time to process and assimilate the information.

Disclosing at work

Our interviewees had a wide range of opinions about disclosure at work. Nick clearly states on his business website that he is autistic. Lyn told me that although she had not yet disclosed at work, she planned to soon, as all of her colleagues were women with experience of working with autistic children and she felt safe telling them that she is autistic. However, she said that when working in previous jobs, she didn't mention it as she didn't generally talk about herself at work. Bridget admitted that she had not come 'out out' at work but that she was beginning to talk about it with people. Nick shared this story:

> About 18 months ago, I finally plucked up the courage to put a post on LinkedIn, to say 'I am autistic'. And the reaction was surprising. I thought it would just fall dead, but actually there was quite a lot of support out there. It's been interesting because some people

who I thought were good friends never made a comment and have never mentioned it. And other people who I barely know made comments and phoned me up, got in touch and said, 'Let's go for a walk.' And the funny thing that came out of it is they said, 'You saying that made me realize, because I thought I was exactly like you, that I'm actually autistic as well.'

Just as disclosing to the people in your personal life is a deeply subjective thing, so is disclosing at work. There's no requirement to disclose being autistic before or after you get a job. It's simply something you may wish to do if you are struggling with some aspect of your working environment. For example, if there is a dress code that would be difficult for you to manage due to sensory issues, or your office has fluorescent lights you find uncomfortably bright, discussing alternative options with your line manager might be helpful.

In the UK, the Equality Act 2010 sees disability as any impairment that has a long-term impact on a person's ability to carry out day-to-day activities. (As an aside, the Act's definition of disability makes no mention whatsoever of having to have a diagnosis.) As such, employers are required by law to provide reasonable adjustments to disabled staff. The clue is in the name: 'reasonable adjustments' are just that. Disclosing to your employer means you may get a quieter working area, a more flexible schedule or even the ability to work from home for some or all of the time. You are unlikely to get a purpose-built office or be able to set your working hours for a time when the rest of your team is unavailable. While this is true for the UK, please check for local information if you're based elsewhere.

Many people don't choose to tell people at work unless and until they are absolutely certain about this being the right choice. In the 1970s, a psychologist called Abraham Maslow devised a pyramid of requirements for a happy life that he called Maslow's Hierarchy of Human Needs.[1] At the bottom of the pyramid are things like food and water, shelter and safety. Just above these most basic needs is belonging. As human beings, we must feel we belong somewhere. It's vital to our happiness and wellbeing.

If a person fits in well at work, disclosure may be very scary as a person might worry how things could change if they talk about being autistic. Where they had once felt a sense of belonging at work, post-disclosure they may not. So, it is a tricky business that must be very carefully managed. It's important to note that you can talk about your sensory issues or communication needs without ever saying that you are autistic. Sometimes it is better to focus on your needs rather than autism itself.

Suzi's thoughts on disclosure

It has taken me a long time to talk openly about being autistic for many of the reasons that Kate explains, and I am sad to say that I still harbour a fear of being judged unfavourably (this is a work in progress, though, and I have come a long way).

Now I am conscious of the reasons for holding back, I am more aware and therefore more able to speak up about being autistic and what it means for me. I also realize that the more I (and others) speak up, the more people can realize that we do exist, we have a lot to contribute and we come in all shapes, sizes and genders.

For me, talking about being autistic (and ADHD) is my soul's purpose and it is my mission to educate both informally and formally and to dispel the myths and stereotypes that are still widely perpetuated.

It is important to remember that to disclose is always a personal choice and that it is OK if you wish to or not. We are all at different places on our journeys and it's so important to take your journey at your pace.

As discussed in Chapter 8: Masking, it can be helpful to be aware that other people's reactions to disclosure are not always helpful, supportive or sensitive. I'm sure you may have already found this out; alternatively, you may have experienced helpful and validating responses, which happens, too – there really are some great people out there.

I have had a range of reactions from acceptance and knowing to dismissal and disbelief, which really hurt at the time. Seventeen years ago, when I first realized I could be autistic, I confided in a colleague because I really trusted her and she had been so supportive of me. I was absolutely shocked by her response!

She said to me, 'You can't be autistic, you are nothing like Roy from *Coronation Street*.' If you are not familiar with Britain's longest-running soap opera, Roy Cropper is an autistically coded character who also happens to be a walking stereotype of the male presentation of autism. Roy is a trainspotting cafe owner who talks in a logical Dr Spock way and often doesn't 'get' jokes.

I was shocked, upset and hurt by her reaction. I was totally unprepared for her response of disbelief and invalidation, and that she compared me to someone so different felt like a betrayal. I was devastated and didn't speak up again for quite a while.

In hindsight, I realize she was not coming from a bad place. She was ignorant about autism, and the only point of reference she had at this time was a fictional character from a TV show and the children she had worked with. The awareness and understanding just was not there yet, especially how autism can present in girls and women.

I have had some positive reactions to disclosure, too, and it's important to highlight these so that the fears can be addressed and overcome, step by step. In my most recent role before becoming self-employed, I told my manager about being autistic and ADHD, and she said something like 'OK, thanks for telling me. How can I best support you?' and I know of many people who have had similar responses. I do appreciate that it can be a gamble, though, and it can be hard to gauge how others might respond.

What I have learned is how important it is to get to know ourselves, our strengths and our challenges and to find the language to express our needs and wants (see Chapter 5: Communication). Confidence is an essential ingredient, as are courage and the willingness to get comfortable or at least be OK with discomfort.

It is also helpful to uncover and identify any beliefs that might be holding you back. For years I held on to the belief that I didn't seem 'autistic enough', which was not serving me at all. It was, in fact, holding me back from speaking my truth.

The great thing about having and owning our truths and reality is that they are ours and no one can take them away from us. Not even the opinions of others, however unhelpful they might be, can damage us when we own our power. When we learn to take back our power, we can proudly own our truth, our reality and our autistic experience and that, my friend, is one of the most empowering things we can do for ourselves and those who will follow in our footsteps.

— Chapter 13 —

Friends

KATE

I really wanted friendships...and relationships, and to really love people as well. My problem is that I just find them exhausting. I find it absolutely exhausting.

KATHARINE

When I was a child, I never had a group of friends. I had one friend at a time, and that friend was always another odd one out, like I was. That friend would be another child who also really struggled with the world, or it would be a bully (who also really struggled with the world, it's fair to say) who took me on as a fall guy for their escapades.

These friendships were short, transient affairs, lasting, at most, an entire school year and then falling apart. I just didn't know how to do friendship, and neither did any of those childhood friends.

As a teenager, I did have a group of friends. I was a goth living in a Midwestern US town. Given there were so few of us, the goths in my school mostly stuck together, and had goth barbecues and nights out. For the first time in my life (and for the last time for a long while after this), I felt I belonged somewhere. This was a powerful feeling. I still didn't know how to be a friend (and was awful at this), but I fitted in simply due to my clothes, hairstyle and taste in music.

This sense of belonging came to a dramatic end when I went

to university. I didn't fit in anywhere and struggled to make any friends at all. After a year, I became very depressed. Unfortunately, as I had no support network around me, I didn't know what was happening to me: that I was depressed and needed help. I didn't seek or receive any mental health support and, in the end, I dropped out of university.

After this, I went through decades of having one friend or a few friends at a time. I confused work friends with real friends. I tried and failed dozens of times to find deep and meaningful connections with people and form friendships.

I came to understand that I am autistic shortly after my daughter was diagnosed. Like many others, my child's autism diagnosis led me to look at my own quirks and difficulties. I started reading about women and Asperger's (as autism without learning disability was then called). I had a lot of lightbulb moments and thought, 'This is me! I'm autistic!'

I was very fortunate at that time that I was running a charity I'd set up to support parents of autistic children. Of course, many of those parents were also autistic (whether or not they knew or acknowledged this). I felt as if I was finally meeting people I really connected with. Over a decade on, many of the people I met at that time are still my very close friends.

What is so hard about friendships?

Friendships are a part of life that we cannot prepare for. We aren't taught how to make friends or be a friend, and it does not come as naturally to us as it seems to do for neurotypical people.

Depictions of friends and friendship groups on television and in films are often over the top and unrealistic. Also, we are unlikely to have watched our parents in one-to-one situations with their friends as these would have happened away from us. We likely won't have had good role models for being friends or even receiving friendship from another person.

Most crucially, when we were children, we didn't know we were autistic. We didn't know why we felt so weird, alien and isolated. Most of us had no idea how to make or keep friends and just bumbled our way through all sorts of social mishaps and sometimes unpleasant situations involving other kids.

Up until the age of around six or seven, children play with toys, and this is how early social bonds form. After this point, most neurotypical children move away from toys and begin socializing and forming friendships based on complex sets of nuanced criteria. This is a painfully difficult time for autistic children, as the gap between themselves and their same-age peers quickly becomes a chasm.

Many of us were and still are left out of things or not invited to social events. Emma shared with me how hurtful it was to find out she had not been invited to parties and weddings when others in her social circle were.

Desperate to fit in

As I discuss in Chapter 8: Masking, most of us will have started masking at a very young age. As such, for most of our lives, we won't have been developing our own personalities or sense of self. Many of us were blown around by social winds and changing trends, tastes and fashions that we will have found very hard to keep up with.

Some of us will have been blessed with one or two precious friendships that have maintained to this day. However, most of us simply blundered our way through our childhood and teen years clueless about how to manage friendships.

Alice told me:

> I just didn't really know how to do friends. So, I did have friends, but never like a big friendship group, which I always really wanted. I just couldn't...people just didn't seem to include me. And I really

struggled with people just sort of disappearing out of my life without explaining, and feeling that I'd done something terribly wrong, but not really understanding what. So, I was very conscious that it was like there was something I was getting wrong, but I wasn't sure what it was, for my whole life.

Some of us also had intense interests in things that weren't mainstream. Or we loved playing with toys or engaging with books and other media that weren't considered 'normal' for our age group. These things will have made it difficult to connect with other people who weren't interested in the same things.

Jeff said:

> I have always had difficulty when interacting with others and have struggled to make and keep friendships. I don't really understand other people very well, especially my own peer group. When I was young, I usually hung out with adults as I liked their predictability. My hobbies and interests were always different from others'.

Our interviewees had very similar experiences and the stories they shared really touched my heart. Sarah told us:

> As a kid, I used to read books about friendships, like the cheerleader series, which was all about groups of girlfriends, then how they interacted. And there's so much that I was reading to try and absorb and learn. And then I would try and be that version of a friend, like, 'That's what friends do'.

HOW TO MAKE FRIENDS

Friends arrive in our lives from all sorts of places. Some people have friends from childhood or school. Some have friends who started as work colleagues. If you are struggling to make friends, here are some ideas.

Look for autistic social groups

I've been working in the field of autism for over a decade. In this time, support for all autistic individuals, from children to adults, has improved in my area. This may not be true everywhere, but it is certainly the case that there are now more people talking about autism than ever before. These discussions create awareness, and awareness creates opportunities for connection.

There may be a social network for autistic adults in your area. Search the internet for 'autistic adult social groups [your area]'. You may find something worth checking out.

It's important to note that autism-related social groups will include a very wide range of people with a very wide range of needs. You may have to try a few different groups to find one that is right for you.

Find a group based on your interests

It might be more productive to find a social group based around your interests. If the interest is very niche, this may just be an online group, and that is OK. Meetup is a great website for finding social groups with specific interests (including groups specifically for autistic adults).*

Take things slowly

When you meet someone you feel you might have a connection with, don't rush into a friendship. This can be difficult, especially if you feel you really 'click' with this person and have a lot in common.

If you've met someone through a social or interest-based

---

* www.meetup.com

group, spend time with them during the group session first. If you've met a different way, ask them to meet you for a coffee or to go for a walk. Let a few weeks pass between each meeting. The reason for this is that if you rush into a friendship with someone and then realize that they are not right for you for some reason, it's easier to end things if you haven't moved too fast in forming the friendship.

Online friendships are valid!
For many reasons, some of us prefer online friendships to in-person friendships. Anxiety, sensory sensitivities and other issues can prevent us from meeting people 'irl' (in real life). If this works best for you, then that is absolutely fine. Connection is connection.

The double empathy conundrum

As mentioned in Chapter 5: Communication, the double empathy theory posits that the difficulties autistic people sometimes have when communicating with non-autistic people are down to a difference in empathy styles. Reciprocal empathy requires that both people have mutual understanding, experiences and similar communication styles. When we don't find this in the person we are communicating with (nor them in us), this can create an issue where neither person feels understood.

This was a common issue for our interviewees. Lauren told me:

> I find that I've become like an over-the-top, kind and thoughtful person. Because I think that's what I need and what I would want from a person, and also what is appropriate. And actually, I think that makes me quite vulnerable as well. It's a kind of social interaction that can be really painful sometimes because I don't understand why someone's doing something that's not very nice.

Autistic people often speak in a very 'face value' way. We say what we mean and can be very direct. Katharine said, 'I think I often say things that accidentally upset people. Because I think a lot of people assume that there's an underlying message to what I'm saying [when there isn't].'

Adding to these complications, some of us struggle to understand facial expressions, tone of voice and body language, and may not use these things in a neurotypical way, either. Alice shared:

> Throughout my life people have been like, oh God, you're so tactless, you're very blunt. So, I think it's more that the bluntness, the problems with eye contact and that I have no patience for people that bore me and I just can't pretend otherwise. So, I think it's just really obvious. Like I just have not so much a resting bitch face, but more sort of resting indifferent face.

WHO IS A FRIEND?

Making connections with others is sometimes fraught with difficulties. It can be hard to work out who is a friend and who is a different type of connection – for example, an acquaintance or a work colleague or someone who has a romantic or sexual interest in us.

I have also had difficulty when it comes to people like therapists and counsellors. In those relationships, I shared so many deep and personal things, and often had a very comfortable rapport with that person. I've had to remind myself that they are not my friend; they are a person acting in a professional capacity.

It can be difficult to work out whether or not a person is a friend. Some of us have people in our lives who have vague and undefined roles. Sometimes we fall in with people because of circumstance (e.g. we work with them, or they are our neighbour).

Here is a short checklist of factors to consider when working out if someone is a friend. You can also use this list for people who are new to your life.

Are they loyal and dependable?
Do they turn up when they say they will? It's fair to say that some neurodivergent people struggle with executive functioning skills, which can impact on punctuality. Here, I'm more specifically referring to a person who consistently breaks plans and lets you down.

Do you have things in common?
A friend is someone you have a lot to talk about with. A lack of common interests or lifestyle choices may be a sign that this person is not long-term friendship material. If nothing else, a friendship must have a foundation of mutual empathy. Without this, it will fall apart.

Is the relationship reciprocal?
Are you always paying for coffees/food/petrol? If you do things to help them, do they in turn do things to help you? If there is a big imbalance here, this person is likely not a friend.

Do you feel good when you are with them?
This is crucial. Anyone who makes you feel uncomfortable in any way, for any reason, is not a friend. Listen to your gut instinct here. If a person makes you feel consistently 'icky', it's time to move away from them.

Do they touch you inappropriately?
A person who touches you or looks at you in a way that makes you feel uncomfortable (even after you have asked them not to) is not a friend.

> **Do you pay them for their services?**
> A counsellor, carer, therapist, personal assistant...these are service people. You may have a friendly relationship, but they are not friends. Anyone you can fire isn't a friend.

It's a quality v quantity issue

Emma said something that really struck home for me. She told me that it's a choice; while she may have fewer friends than some other people, the connections are deeper and of a far higher quality. I agree with this wholeheartedly. Now in my fifties, I have two very close friends, a handful of slightly less close friends and then lots of acquaintances. These connections create a solid emotional safety net for me.

This is an important concept for us as late-discovered autistic adults to grasp – that there's no minimum acceptable quantity of close friends. I believe that as long as we have even one person we can truly be ourselves with, that is a good start. Emma mentioned to me that she'd been to a wedding where there were ten bridesmaids. We both laughed and wondered, 'Who has that many friends?'

Like attracts like

There is an interesting phenomenon that exists when it comes to neurodivergent individuals: we seem to unconsciously attract each other. When I was setting up the charity and making new friends, I didn't recognize until much later that almost all of them were neurodivergent in some way. Several of our interviewees commented on this as well, that friends they've had since childhood have also recently learned that they are autistic.

Why does this happen? I don't have a scientific answer; I can only give my own experience. First, it goes back to the double empathy issue I mentioned above. We connect with other autistic people because we will often have had comparable past experiences and we may have similar perspectives on life.

I find with my friends (who are all knowingly or presumably autistic) that we don't have to explain things in the same way we would with non-neurodivergent people. We can speak in a sort of shorthand. We just 'get' each other in a way I can't quite explain.

Not wishing to sound elitist, but it may be the case that we make more complex connections between things that only other autistic people would get. We may also have more obscure, specific and/or non-mainstream interests that would attract other autistic people. Again, this is not a scientific explanation! These are just things I have come to understand as an autistic in the world.

You are not boring

It's very common for autistic people to feel unconfident when it comes to making friends. I have had a very interesting and full life, but I still feel I am fairly boring and struggle with making new friends. I know I am not alone in this kind of thinking.

I feel the way around this is to be with people you have something in common with. That could be a specific interest or a lifestyle. For example, most of my friends are not only autistic but have autistic children, so this alone gives us a huge amount to talk about.

What we really need, especially as we get older, is people who are as interested in the minutiae of our lives as we are in theirs. We need at least one friend who wants to hear about our new vacuum cleaner, that we were excited to find cherries on special offer at Lidl and that we've added something new to our collection of whatever it is we collect. To this person or these people, we are far from boring. We comfort them with our tales of day-to-day life.

— Chapter 14 —

Love and Sex

KATE

Until my mid-thirties, I masked my way into every romantic relationship I had. I had an intense need to be loved and so did everything in my power to influence potential romantic partners. I would meet a man and get to know everything about him. I would then morph into his perfect woman. I'd take on his hobbies and interests and essentially do whatever he wanted me to. This was, as you can imagine, extremely unhealthy and at times very damaging. It was also an extremely dishonest way to behave.

I could maintain the facade for a few years, but then it would all fall apart as I could not keep up that level of intensive masking. The relationship would end and the man would be hurt and bewildered – how could I have been one person for so long (the 'perfect partner') and then become another (my real self) when I stopped masking?

I've had countless relationships, including several marriages and divorces. My romantic worldview changed dramatically when I realized that I am autistic. I stopped masking and instead allowed myself to be fully present and 100 per cent myself in my romantic relationships. This can be hard. It means I now push back on things I don't want or don't like. I ask difficult questions, and I ask for what I want and need. I've had to end relationships that weren't a good fit.

On the positive side, I have had truly gorgeous experiences. I know what my sensory and sexual desires are and ensure that these are met. My current partner (easily the most neurodivergent man I have ever met) is my perfect match. I can be truly myself with him and he meets all of my relationship-based needs. There is no stress or drama with this person, which frees up a huge amount of brain space for other things.

Romantic love and sexual relationships can be very difficult for autistic people. The challenges outlined in every other chapter are all present when it comes to romantic love and sex. Communication, sensory sensitivities, RSD... It really is no wonder that many of us struggle here.

This is the last chapter I wrote for this book (although it appears earlier in the running order) and it has been the hardest to write. I'm sharing my very personal experiences with you. I'm also providing several references for further exploration. I want you to know that whatever you are feeling, thinking or going through with regard to gender, sex and relationships is OK. Whatever is normal for you is great. I hope by being open about my own life, you can feel a bit less weird (if 'weird' is where you are at right now).

Interestingly, when we asked our interviewees for the topics that they wanted to discuss, only one chose 'love and sex'. I think we all have strong feelings about romantic love and sex, and have had our fair share of pain, confusion and hardship in this area.

Belonging, romance and intimacy

Both Suzi and I have mentioned a few times in this book our human need for belonging. However we present from a gender and/or sexuality perspective, we all need to feel we belong somewhere. How we each meet this need is very individual.

The Cambridge Dictionary definition of 'romantic' is: 'relating to love or a close relationship'. Love can take many forms. A close relationship could be any type of relationship. Note that there is no reference to passion or sex in this definition. This is an important distinction: romance is all about love and closeness. Whatever else happens is up to you and your partner, if you choose to have one.

I have a primal need to be in a partnership with a man. I know this about myself on a deep, intrinsic level. However, I have female friends who do not feel this way and are very happy on their own. In fact, one of my friends told me that she has consciously let go of a need for sex.

In addition to belonging, we all need intimacy. This does not mean we require physical touch, as some of us do not have this need. Intimacy takes many forms. For you, intimacy may be a close relationship with someone where you both know each other extremely well and thus can cater for each other's specific desires.

What is love?

In Chapter 7: Emotions, I share that I feel emotions on an intense level. When I love someone, there are no half measures. I love BIG. I am also a person who falls in love easily, and in the past, I regularly confused love with lust.

I remember years ago searching the internet for something like 'How do I know if I love someone?' I was experiencing all sorts of feelings for someone I'd only recently met. The answer that came back said something along the lines of, 'You love someone when you can't stop thinking about them, and you care about their wellbeing.' I was left none the wiser.

Love for autistic individuals is dependent on several factors. If you are someone who cannot easily identify your emotions, knowing whether or not you love someone will be difficult. For me, I know I love someone when I can trust them entirely. I can be myself with them, and we have things in common, especially common life experiences.

I feel love as a physical sensation, but you may not. I feel 'love' for my friends and my partner. In my body, this feels like a warm, comforting sensation in my chest. For my daughter and my partner, I also feel 'in love'. Being in love is a sensation I have in my tummy; it's a deep, sweet, delicious feeling.

If you are struggling to work out your feelings for someone, this in itself is a sign that you have a connection with that person that may be different from what you have with someone who is just a friend. You may find that writing about or talking to a friend about how you are feeling helps. Searching the internet for 'autistic love' brings up a wide range of interesting resources that you may find useful as well.

Sensory differences and sex

Our unique sensory profiles create rich and interesting backdrops for sex and touch. Some of us find extreme sensory delight in being in close physical and/or sexual contact with another person. Their scent, the feel of their skin, the sound of their voice and so on can fulfil deep needs within us. The actual physical impact of sex can also be intensely satisfying for some of us (beyond the pleasure of sex in itself).

On the flipside, some of us can find sexual touch extremely difficult. The sensory aspects of another body might be overwhelming. Another person's cosmetics, fragrance, shampoo, washing powder, fabric softener might be unbearable. Over- or under-sensitive genitals can also be an issue for some autistic adults.

We can find ourselves with partners who have opposite needs to ours. Bill told me that he struggles as he needs a great deal more physical affection than his wife does:

> I crave physical affection and I think that's because I don't have emotional sensation [Bill is alexithymic]. And affection, be it touch, a hug, kiss, or whatever brings a sensation. Not an internal sensation, a skin sensation. I'm just beginning to think and understand how I can deal with that in a positive and productive

way. It's been an interesting thought to have had, that probably the reason I need physical attention is because I don't have emotional sensation.

He went on to say that he doesn't want to have an affair. He's working out how he can get his needs met in a safe way.

We need to do it our way

As autistic adults, we need to live our day-to-day lives in a way that aligns with our emotional, physical and sensory needs. Similarly, our experience of love and sex must be on our terms. I find that understanding my needs as an autistic woman has, in many ways, helped me to design an essentially bespoke package with my current partner.

This is your prerogative, too. Your needs are valid. If you don't have what you need from a romantic and/or sexual perspective, you can find ways to change your current situation. This is an area where we need to see the grey and not just the black and white. It doesn't have to be all (with that person) or nothing (not with that person). There may be a middle ground (working things out and improving the situation with that person) that is worth exploring.

DATING APPS

I have met my last several partners via a wide variety of dating apps. I have found this an efficient way to meet people, and I've learned a lot along the way about how best to approach using these apps.

The pictures

Every dating app will have you upload a picture. It's best to upload two or three. Ensure that the pictures are recent – within the past two years. If you don't have a recent picture, take some selfies with your phone over a few days. If possible, ask a friend for help with taking and choosing the best picture(s).

The words
The dating app profile is a way for you to share the most relevant things about yourself. Some tips:

- Be honest and genuine.
- Be positive. Don't mention your ex or any negative past experiences.
- Keep it short and sweet – no more than two or three short paragraphs.
- Avoid being 'jokey'; be straightforward and direct.
- Write about what you are like as a person and what your interests are.

If you don't know how to describe yourself, enlist the help of a friend with this bit, too.

The investment
Some dating apps offer a free option, but these tend to be very limited in functionality. As autistics, we can be a bit all-or-nothing, but I advise against paying for more than a month at first. You never know what could happen (I met my current partner on the first day of joining a dating app) and you don't want to be stuck paying for months of a dating app you no longer want or need.

Take a businesslike approach
Engaging with dating apps requires a businesslike mindset. You will very likely (and very quickly) feel the sting of rejection if you message or like someone and they don't message or like you back. Don't take this personally; it's about them, not you.

If you start to interact with someone and it feels as if it's going somewhere, plan to meet. Messaging for ages can create a very distorted mental view of the other person and can lead to huge disappointment. It's best to meet early on to ensure that they are as good as they seem in writing.

Safety first
Don't give out too much information. After messaging for a few days, arrange to meet in a public place, like a pub or cafe. Tell a friend that you are going to meet someone and when and where you are going to meet that person. Agree to text or ring your friend when you get home.

I don't mean to be patronizing with what might feel like obvious advice. A few years ago, I put myself in a very dangerous situation because I got excited about meeting someone new. Safety went out of the window. I am reminding you to be safe because it's easy to forget ourselves when we get caught up in the excitement of a potential new relationship.

Disclosure
In my experience, it is not necessary to disclose being autistic or neurodivergent on a dating profile. As I mention in Chapter 13: Friends, autistic people tend to naturally gravitate towards each other. This has been consistently true for me when using dating apps. I've always ended up with someone who is neurodivergent in some way.

Take your time
Finding a new partner isn't easy. It may take you a long time to find someone, or you may connect very quickly with someone wonderful. Take your time, and if it doesn't work for you, leave it and try again in six months.

The perfect partnership

If you are in a relationship, one of several things is happening. It might be the perfect partnership, with open communication about all things. It might be the entirely wrong relationship, where there is abuse and mistrust. Or it could be a good-enough relationship that, with some work, can become much better.

I have always found the work of Eva A. Mendes very helpful in my relationships. Eva writes about autism, relationships and sexuality. I highly recommend her book *Armchair Conversations on Love and Autism: Secrets of Happy Neurodiverse Couples*.[1] This is a collection of interviews with neurodivergent (and neurotypical) people talking about how and why their relationships work. It includes people of a variety of genders, ethnic backgrounds and sexual orientations.

This book is a useful reminder of the fact that we can all find love. For us, it may look entirely unique and very different from society's standard vision of relationships. The way we interact and present, and the way we choose to have sex (or don't, as the case may be) will be completely exclusive to us and our chosen partner(s).

Gender diversity

A 2020 study on gender diversity[2] found that autistic people are three to six times more likely than neurotypical people not to identify with the gender they were born with. This feels true in my own experience as well. While I currently present as a very feminine female, in the past my gender has been very fluid and has veered at times to the masculine.

There are many, many ways to express gender. The number of possible different gender identities, at the time of writing, is difficult to ascertain. We are in an exciting time with regard to gender identity as a lot of people are talking about it! I found Wikipedia's list of gender identities[3] interesting and useful. This is another area where each of us can choose a unique and individual path for ourselves.

Sexuality

Our sexual orientation is also very unique and personal to us. A 2021 study[4] found that autistic adults are eight times more likely than neurotypical people to choose a sexual orientation other than heterosexual.

How cool are we, choosing our gender and sexuality to meet our needs and preferences! Eva A. Mendes has also written a book on this topic with Meredith R. Maroney.[5] *Gender Identity, Sexuality and Autism* may be of interest to you if you are exploring these aspects of yourself.

Kinky boots

Further to choosing different paths for gender and sexuality, it would appear that autistic adults are more likely to engage in bondage, discipline (or dominance), sadism and masochism (BDSM) and kink. In my own personal experience, being this way inclined myself, most people that I have met in this community are neurodivergent. Although there is very little solid research on this topic, a small 2023 study[6] discusses at length why this might be. We love predictability and many of us need routines. Some of us may also find comfort in rituals. BDSM play and kink provide outlets for us to enjoy and explore these things.

Communication

It may sound trite but the key to great relationships and great sex is communication. Asking for what you want and need is vital. Being assertive and setting boundaries to protect yourself (see Chapter 5: Communication, and Chapter 8: Masking for more on this) are also incredibly important.

For many years, I was with a partner I could not talk to. He would shut down any discussion that involved working out the problems in our relationship. Still, I persevered. I naively thought that, in time, things would get better. Needless to say, they never did. I am now with a partner where the communication is wide open and free flowing. This is how it must be for all of us, especially as we are autistic and have such very specific needs.

You don't have to be lonely

While I have had a lot of romantic relationships, I have also gone through periods of intense loneliness. At times, the loneliness was so extreme that it felt like a presence in itself.

Loneliness is a killer.[7] It can take a great toll on our mental and physical health. I know from painful experience that it is possible to feel lonely in a crowded room, or sitting next to your partner. However, loneliness is a solvable problem.

Every romantic relationship must have a foundation of friendship. See Chapter 13: Friends for ideas on how to get started with meeting new people.

It's up to you

You decide what is right for you. It's never too late to explore new avenues or try new things. Most of my sexual identity is based on experiences I have had from my late forties onwards.

Whether or not you choose to have a partner or to have sex is entirely up to you. This again is one of the great things about being autistic. We dance to our own unique beat.

— **Part 4** —

THE FUTURE IS BRIGHT!

— Chapter 15 —

Passions and Interests

SUZI

When you really ask [someone] about their deep interest, there's something magical that happens. Yeah. It's something truly, truly magical.

IRENE

A wonderful part of being autistic for me is the absolute wonder and intensity of interests and passions that capture the heart and imagination. These are often called 'special interests', a term I am not massively keen on. If a neurotypical person has a deep interest, they are called an 'expert'. For autistic folks, it's called a 'special interest'. For me, it feels too 'other' and the energy of the two terms feels very different. However, you of course use whichever terminology resonates with you.

Morwenna agreed when she said:

I know it's the intensity and the passion of the interests [that autistic people have] that is different and that's what meets the diagnostic criteria, but that over-medicalizing of it in that kind of way bothers me, and I sometimes just say, actually, 'I've got expertise in this.'

ALL ABOUT MONOTROPISM

How can autistic folks focus so intently on their passions and interests?

It's long been known that autistic people have intense areas of passion and interest, and monotropism is a theory that was independently formulated by Dinah Murray and Wenn Lawson.[1] Later, Mike Lesser worked alongside them both to develop, apply and explain the theory.

So, what is it?

Monotropism is a neuro-affirming theory that helps to describe and make sense of the intense passions experienced by autistic folks and the narrow focus of attention on these passions.

It is now known that the flow of attention is different in autistic minds and therefore it is much harder to switch tasks and transition between activities, conversations and tasks, and so on. What is needed in these moments is time and space to make those transitions as smooth as possible, as well as self-compassion for your needs that are important and valid.

If you find yourself rushing between tasks (hello ADHD) and feeling stressed and overwhelmed, then it might be that you need more time between tasks or activities to give your brain time to process the change and feel ready for the next thing.

Monotropic (as opposed to polytropic) people experience an almost tunnel-style vision when engaged in an area of interest, which can lead to a flow state that is all encompassing. It can lead to pleasure, deep learning and the acquisition of new skills.

As with many things, environment plays a major role in whether monotropic folks thrive or become dysregulated.

PASSIONS AND INTERESTS

Think of a busy open-plan office where people stop by your desk and ask for a 'quick chat' or, worse, start 'talking at you' mid-task!

Often it is the autistic person who is judged unfairly when this happens, with others assuming they are 'rude', 'disinterested', 'rigid' or even 'anti-social'.

Do you ever feel annoyed or even angry when someone interrupts you when you are fully engaged in a task or activity that you are enjoying? I know I do, and the more intensely passionate I feel, the more annoyed I will be when interrupted.

Monotropism may well describe my challenges around umpiring and refereeing when I was a PE teacher all those years ago. I remember this aspect of the job being one of the things I hated about teaching. I didn't know why, I just believed that I was crap at umpiring.

I have a vivid memory of umpiring a netball tournament and the players stopped play and shouted to me, 'Are you going to blow the whistle? I clearly travelled.' Oops, I had completely missed that because there was so much activity going on and my focus was not on the feet of the players. My goodness, it's not surprising that I struggled with so many aspects of teaching, is it?

On a serious note, though, the impact of these situations was huge and took a devastating toll on my self-esteem and confidence. In that moment, I felt stupid, ashamed and embarrassed. I was supposed to be a PE teacher, and I couldn't even do my job. Or so my inner critic told me. Thankfully, I am now very forgiving of my challenges, and it really does help to know there are reasons for them.

It's important to understand how monotropism may affect you, your responses and your relationships. There is nothing wrong with you – it is another example of how your wonderful brain is wired.

Traditionally, much of the outdated information about autism suggests that autistic people are a) boys and b) 'trainspotters' or 'little professors', which has done very little to help autistic people. The autistic people interviewed for this book have a wide and varied range of interests and passions that do not fit society's expectations of what it means to be autistic. Of her interests, Klaudia said, 'I love to read, I love to write poetry, I love art. Art makes me a better person.' In this chapter, a variety of interests are discussed which demonstrate the diversity among us unique autistic humans.

It is important to remember that your passions are your passions, and whether they are present throughout your life or stay for a little while then completely disappear, that is OK. Many autistic and ADHD folk report that they can be hugely passionate about something for weeks, months or even years and suddenly the interest has gone, just like that.

As an autistic ADHDer, this has been the story of my life. When I was a child, I would get really into a sport – for example, tennis, then football. I would beg and plead with my parents to buy me all the equipment that accompanied each sport. They would dutifully take me along to training and then I would suddenly not want to go anymore.

I was lucky in that I was never made to feel bad about my fleeting interests. It was how it was, and now I look back with such fondness and gratitude that I was fortunate enough to have parents who accepted my ways and my interests. I even have a birthday card from when I was about 12 years old showing an untidy bedroom and, again, it was received and delivered (I think) with love and humour and, as I understand it, acceptance.

The benefits of deep passions and interests

For so many autistic people, passions are an important and integral part of life. Many report a feeling of safety and escape when pursuing their interests, and the positive benefits on mental health and wellbeing must not be underestimated.

PASSIONS AND INTERESTS

Passions and interests can also be interwoven with identity, and fictional characters have been a source of inspiration and connection for many. To be able to identify with someone in a world where it can seem as if you are alone and different is, to put it mildly, very comforting.

Morwenna talked about the often-transient nature of passions:

> Mine kind of wax and wane a bit, but music has been a real passion. So, I play acoustic guitar and just picking that up, I can lose time over that, which is just brilliant, and that gorgeous sort of state of flow is so exquisite for me.

When people don't understand, and the shame can set in

As already mentioned, the passions and interests of autistic folk are wide and varied. Sometimes they can be perceived and judged as odd or obscure, which can lead to feelings of shame and embarrassment. These are not nice ways to feel, especially about things that bring so much joy and pleasure, as well as the ability to satiate the appetite of learning. Irene explained:

> I did fall into the rabbit hole of World War II and Hitler and the whole shebang. Not because I was a fan of Hitler, of course not, but he was a fascinating, interesting man to understand. Because I didn't understand his actions, I needed to understand the 'why' behind it, and I've had my sister making fun of me a lot throughout the years because of it.

This is an example of what might be judged as obscure, and I bet some people might even deem it an 'inappropriate' interest (which is rubbish by the way) for a young girl (she was a teenager at the time). Irene's example gives insight into how autistic minds are driven to find out 'why', and this is a magnificent strength in my opinion. To question and seek answers is a valuable trait to have and, of course, has led to amazing discoveries throughout time.

Irene's example also shows that often our interests and passions drive us as if by an inner force. No matter what others say about our interests and passions, we keep learning about them regardless. This shows tenacity and determination – incredible strengths that can be tapped into in many different scenarios.

Of being made fun of by her sister for her interest in Hitler, Irene said, 'I felt very hurt at the time, and I think I just cried in my room.' So many times, I have seen people roll their eyes when an autistic person has attempted to connect and share via their passionate interests, and it makes me so sad. I learned a long time ago to keep quiet and to 'tone down' my sharing of my interests such as autism and ADHD due to others' eye rolls, sighs and changes in tone of voice. We autistic folk are extremely aware of and pick up on even the slightest change in someone else's tone.

It is often said that autistics can sense other people's energy, and the slight shifts and changes in them can throw us off balance and leave us feeling confused and frustrated.

SETTING PROTECTIVE BOUNDARIES AROUND YOUR PASSIONS AND INTERESTS

When other people are judgemental or making fun of you and your interests, Irene advised, 'Embrace your passions and set boundaries around the people who do those things.'

Ideas for what to say if someone comments unfavourably about your passions and interests

- 'This is really important to me and brings me a lot of joy, so I will continue to find out all I can about it.'

- 'My interests are important to me and form my values. I am happy to pursue them.'
- 'I feel upset when people make fun of my passions and interests, so please stop.'
- 'Yes, I know this subject is a bit different from what everyone else is interested in, and that is OK, I am happy to be different.'
- 'This is of such interest to me; would you like to know more?'
- 'Thanks for your opinion, but I am going to carry on as this is important to me.'

Questions to ask yourself when people question your passions and interests

- Is this person a good friend to me?
- Whose opinion is most important here?
- What do I believe about myself and my interests? Are there any beliefs that are holding me back? See Chapter 18: Thoughts, Beliefs and the Inner Critic for more guidance on this.
- Who can I speak to openly and honestly about my interests?
- Where can I find people who understand or have similar interests?

Ultimately, you are important here, and your passions are most likely vital to your wellbeing. You are 100 per cent entitled to immerse yourself in them as you wish. Unfortunately, many people are quick to judge and often have good intentions when they offer their words of wisdom. They are likely projecting their own fears and experiences on to you; therefore, it is not even about you, it's about them!

Irene summed this concept up beautifully when she said:

> Remember that what that person says is not a reflection of you, but a reflection of the person saying those words. Your passions are important because they're important to you, and do not let anyone take those passions away from you. Those passions create joy, so treasure them.

A passion shared is a passion doubled

To share your passions with others who appreciate them (and you) can be of great benefit. To feel a sense of connection and belonging is very much a human need and is necessary for survival as well as for living a purposeful and fulfilling life.

Michelle said, 'For me, it's just to allow. Allow passions and interests and find your people.' She continued:

> To find communities of interest is really useful. There are more and more spaces to allow us to monologue about our passions and interests, whether that's on TikTok, or various social media. Or you on Facebook talking on camera to yourself about your passions, because talking about them and exploring verbally is sometimes just as soothing and lovely as doing the interest.

A great book to read is *The Four Agreements* by Don Miguel Ruiz.[2] One of the agreements is 'Don't take anything personally', which sounds difficult, and is! However, once absorbed and embodied, this concept is amazing at releasing any suffering that is occurring due to other people's opinions. When we can truly understand and accept that whatever anyone says or does is about them and not us, we can start to be free from many of the frustrations and upsets that 'other people' have caused us.

By now you might be thinking, 'Why wouldn't we take things personally? We have spent our lives being made to feel odd, somehow wrong, not good enough.' If you are thinking something like that, you are right. Being sensitive souls, we will likely have internalized these projections of society's version of 'normal' and never lived up to them. It is impossible to live up to a set of standards that just do not work for us. It's no wonder that us autistic folk have absorbed and interpreted these messages as there being something wrong with us.

So, I get why it is difficult to believe that nothing is personal and that what others do or say reflects on them and not you, but I wish for you to know that it is the truth.

In her book *Playing Big*, Tara Mohr[3] also talks about the opinions of others being just that, their opinions. Opinions are not fact, and the person who is likely to know the facts is you. At the end of the day, the only person whose opinion matters is your own. I wish I had known this years ago!

Kate's thoughts on interests and passions

I have not had many interests or passions over my lifetime. In fact, sometimes this has made me feel 'not autistic enough' as it seems to be such an autistically aligned thing. I am interested in a lot of different subjects, but I don't retain information easily, so I can't say I have any specialist knowledge about anything. I don't have an issue with the term 'special interest' so I am going to use that here.

For some of us, our partner is our special interest. I know this was true for me with my ex-partner, and I have heard from other autistic women that this has been the case for them as well. For some of us, it's our children, or issues to do with our children – for example, special educational needs and disabilities education law.

Speaking for myself, I also think that my efficient autistic side cancels out my more impulsive ADHD side. The ADHD part of me might think, 'Let's take up weight training!' but my autistic side thinks, 'No way – we simply don't have the space for all that equipment.' This may be true for you, as well.

The point I am making is that if you are like me and don't have any great passion or hobby or special interest, this is totally OK and doesn't mean you are any less autistic than someone who does. Many different factors make us autistic and whether or not you have a special interest plays a very minor role in diagnostic criteria.

— Chapter 16 —

Getting to Know Yourself

KATE

It is extremely common for late-discovered autistic adults to feel as if they don't know themselves at all. I know from personal experience that this can be very disconcerting. Here we are, adults in our thirties, forties, fifties or beyond, and many of us don't know what we enjoy doing, what kinds of food we like to eat or what clothing we like to wear. This can make us feel vulnerable and untethered, because if we don't know ourselves, how do we know that the decisions we've made about our current life circumstances are right? This is very unnerving and can actually be quite scary.

Why does this happen?

As discussed in Chapter 8: Masking, as autistic children, many of us intuitively and intrinsically understood that in the eyes of at least some of the people around us, there was something unacceptable about us. This may have only been at school, or only when in the company of certain relatives, or it may have been a pervasive feeling that we carried with us everywhere. We will have, without even giving it much thought or understanding why, slowly but surely, become someone else. We'll have spent a lot of time – again, this was often unconscious – watching those around us and taking on their mannerisms, interests, clothing choices, taste in music, books and films, and so on.

It's important to explain this here, as *this is why we have no idea who we are*. We have spent most of our lives literally being someone else. Perhaps we became the Funny One, the Clever One or the Perfect One, as many of us, myself included, felt pressured to become. These false roles are deeply, deeply embedded within us; they are in every cell. This is why it is so very disconcerting to realize it was all – or mostly all – a lie.

I have good news!

You are going to go through a very uncomfortable period while you come to terms with, and work to unpick, what is real about your personality and what isn't, and what you like and dislike. Before I go any further, I need to share something that will soften the blow of these harsh realizations. What I have found to be true is that underneath all of the masking and pretending, there is a real you that has always been good. Truly, genuinely good. And that part of you is still within you and always will be.

Your real, core self is like a tenacious buoy that has been repeatedly pulled to the bottom of the ocean, but bounces back up every time. Nothing can keep your core self down. It is your true North. It doesn't matter that you may have been pretending to love bowling or camping or classical music or even heterosexual sex all of these years. Your true, core self is good.

When I learned in my forties that I am autistic, I went through about two years of soul searching to work out what I really wanted and needed, what I wanted to keep and what I needed to let go of. What I realized during this process is that not everything in my life was fake. My core qualities were 100 per cent genuine, and had been with me all my life. Among other things, I have always been intelligent, thoughtful, very creative, affectionate, loving, generous and deeply principled.

I found it comforting to understand that these qualities make up the foundation of the Real Kate. The wild winds of masking may toss everything around on the surface, but I have always had, and will always have, these core, real parts of myself to fall back on.

Start here

It can take some time to find yourself once you recognize that you are autistic. It's important to stay grounded during this time and look at one part of your life at a time. You'll need to be very mindful of the fact that we are generally all-or-nothing, black-and-white thinkers. The urge to change everything at once can be overwhelming. Please resist this. If you rush into changing everything straight away, you will cause yourself a huge amount of stress.

What do you actually like?

Here is a gentle place to start – a simple list of basic questions you can ask yourself. I urge you to spend time with this as the answers may surprise you:

- What are your favourite scents?
- What tastes and flavours do you love?
- What places feed your soul?
- What sounds soothe and ground you?
- What kind of music do you enjoy?
- What are your favourite textures?
- What kind of house do you want to live in?
- What do you love to look at?
- Who are your favourite people to spend time with?

It can be equally useful to do the inverse of this exercise, and ask yourself what you don't like in each of these categories.

When I first did this exercise, I was surprised at what I learned about myself. For example, I had thought that I had a sweet tooth. (I am overweight, and throughout my life, the people around me have commented that I must have a sweet tooth; this opinion clearly went in.) However, when I really looked at it, I acknowledged that the opposite is true: I have a savoury tooth! I much prefer sharp flavours – lemon, dark chocolate, strong cheese, olives, red wine and so on. Similarly, I had thought that my ideal home would be a cosy, cluttered country cottage. On closer inspection, I saw that I prefer the exact opposite of this – my ideal home would actually be a minimalist glass and metal box.

It's important to note that these things will change over time, and new things will be added to the list. When I first went through these questions, my favourite scents were Nag Champa incense and lemon. A few years later, I discovered that I love Palo Santo essential oil, and that went on the list. So, it's useful to keep hold of your answers and think them through every few years to ensure that you are still feeding your soul with the things you love most.

Becoming your real self is going to really, seriously annoy people

As you go through the process of getting to know yourself, you will naturally begin to redraw your boundary lines. Perhaps you've been eating big Sunday roasts with your whole family every week for all of your life, but you've now realized that you actually hate these meals and everything they entail. You will need to make a decision about what to do here: will you stop taking part in these meals altogether, or is there a compromise? Perhaps you can go just for the pudding, or just for a cup of tea and a chat before the big meal. It may indeed be the case that you cannot cope with any of it, and this is fine, too.

An example of this for me is meals with a partner's family (which for me have always been painful reminders of big family meals I endured as a child). I have had countless, agonizing, boring and uncomfortable lunches and dinners with various family members of various ex-partners. I now make it clear to new partners that this really isn't my thing, and that I may choose not to do this.

Similarly, I recently made a new friend who is really into rugby. I have never been to a rugby game or even watched rugby on television. My friend is part of a large, social rugby community and really wants me to come to a game. I explained very clearly that I will go along but as it's very new to me, I might be anxious, I might be very quiet and a bit anti-social, and my friend's friends might just think I'm a bit weird. Sometimes we just need to explain to people what is happening for us.

About a year ago, I dramatically changed my wardrobe. I had got stuck in the idea that women over 40 should wear black and other dark colours (I honestly don't know where this came from for me, but this belief ran deep). In true autistic, all-or-nothing fashion, I got rid of literally all of my black and dark coloured clothing (and there was a lot!) and replaced it with brightly coloured tops, dresses and jumpers. Out went the black leggings and in came jeans. Jeans! I had not worn jeans in over ten years.

Wearing these new colourful clothes feels amazing. When I started wearing bright colours, I felt like myself for the first time. I feel lighter and happier in these brightly coloured things. My autistic daughter, however, cannot cope with this change at all. There are a few of the tops and cardigans that she literally will not allow me to wear. So, I have to be respectful of her needs here and only wear those when I am not around her.

On a more weighty note, all of my family live in the United States. When I was still in contact with them, for many, many reasons, I did not visit them. Sensory issues, financial issues, work, childcare, emotions...all mixed to create a heavy cocktail that made it impossible. This, of course, upset a great many people, not least my elderly parents and sister. I just couldn't, and so I didn't, and I had to manage within myself the consequences of this choice.

You will also find things in your life that, once you realize they are not right for you, have to go. It may be that you've gone out drinking with friends every Friday, but have decided this really isn't something you enjoy. It's possible that you have been a vegetarian or vegan for years because of someone's long-ago influence but now see that what you really want is steak, steak and more steak. Or maybe it's something much bigger, like your relationship with your partner is sadly not working for you.

One useful tool to use in determining whether or not to do something is to ask, 'Will I have to mask in this situation?' Will you need to become someone else in order to get through it (as I did with the meals with in-laws)? If the answer is 'yes', then it might be detrimental to you. Another good rule of thumb when it comes to whether or not you should do a thing is to think about how much recovery time you will need afterwards. If the recovery time (days) will take longer than the actual event (hours), then you might want to decide against it.

Whatever path you choose with these new decisions, the people around you may well be less than pleased. You will ruffle feathers, sometimes a little and sometimes in a huge way. This is OK. What other people – including your parents, siblings and friends – want or need is not more important than what you want or need. (Similarly, what you want and need is not more important than what others want and need, so compromise will be important, too.)

It's OK to fuck shit up

I want to really drive home the point I made in the previous paragraph: *what other people want and need is not more important than what you want and need.* When you start letting your real self out to play, it's probably going to upset people. The people in your life were comfortable with your status quo. They liked the predictable, same-y you, the one that always cooked the entire Christmas meal for 18 people, the one who babysat at short notice, the one that could be counted on to go golfing, hiking or just generally *behave*. You are no longer this person.

It will be painful and uncomfortable to change and be more of what you want and need to be. Friends and family members may not appreciate this. In fact, if the changes you make are remarkable, they may think you've entirely lost the plot. They may become very worried about you. They may think (and loudly and regularly tell you) that you have a mental health issue. They may just get angry because you are messing with their own routine. How dare you do what you want to do when they want you to do something else?

Becoming your true autistic self might be a bit like setting off a bomb in your own life. It will be messy. Things will fly up in the air and land in different places from where they started. This is fine. In fact, this is wonderful. You are taking control of your life and everything in it. You are deciding what stays and what must go. The chaos will eventually recede.

As adults, we are responsible for ourselves. We are in charge of our physical and mental wellbeing. No one else is responsible for these things.

> **REMOVING TOXIC PEOPLE FROM YOUR LIFE**
>
> I remember once having to leave a partner for good, after what had been a toxic, on-again, off-again type of relationship. The things that led me to finally end things are not important here. The bottom line is that the relationship was and always had been bad for me. Being with that person made me feel as if I was never good/pretty/nice/sexy enough. I couldn't be myself with him; I always had to be 'on' and someone I thought he wanted me to be (though I was never entirely sure who that was).

Later, I cut a member of my family out of my life. The recovery process from my relationship with my ex-partner had made me realize one crucial fact: I would never have let someone treat me the way he did if other people hadn't treated me the same way. I stayed with him because the way he treated me was familiar – comfortable even. This made me feel a bit sick.

Just as with my ex-partner, I was never good enough for this family member. I was never thin enough, never had the right job or the right husband or lived in the right place.

I had come to the idea of cutting them out of my life several times before I finally did it. I knew that if I stayed in a relationship with them, there would be two unhappy people, but if I broke ties with them, there would just be one (and it wasn't me).

Cutting people out of your life is scary and hard. Before I did this, I worried about things such as what would happen to me and what people would think of my decision. I worried that telling people I'd cut off this person would be as shocking as saying I'd cut off my own arm.

In the end, I realized I only needed to tell the people closest to me. They all understood and were very supportive.

I thought I would have some sort of breakdown over the loss of this person, but I never did. Letting go of them was more like leaving an awful job I'd had my whole life that I was terrible at and that I'd never enjoyed. It's been freeing and liberating.

Recovering from my relationship with my ex-partner has been far more painful. As I write, some of the wounds still feel fresh. However, I have a wonderful new partner and things are looking up!

You may find that, for your sanity and wellbeing, you may need to let go of some of the people in your life. I'm sharing my story here so that you know it can be done and you will survive it. Letting go of bad people makes room for wonderful new ones.

Try new things

It can be difficult for some of us to try new things. However, this is vital in the search for our real selves. 'If you always do what you always did, you'll always get what you always got' is a useful saying here. If we don't try new things, we might stay very comfortable, but we might miss out on some truly rewarding and life-enhancing experiences.

My ex-partner and I visited a lot of gardens, museums and castles. I had never done these things before but found that I loved them and continue to do these things even though that relationship is over. Similarly, I have lived alone for about six years now, which I had never done before. I now know that this really suits me.

Is there something you've always wanted to do? See if you can take some steps – even small ones – towards trying some of them. For example, if it's a new activity or sport, have a look at some websites about it. Find out what's involved, what equipment you might need, what it costs and so on. You don't need to jump in and actually do the thing (unless you want to). You can gently ease yourself in by simply learning more about it.

You might not like everything you try. As I mentioned earlier, sometimes we do things because the people we spend time with like these things. It can take some time to work out what *you* really like as opposed to what you want to try because your partner or a friend wants to. Take time to give this some considered thought.

What gives you joy?

Similar to working out our favourite things, determining what gives us joy is very helpful in figuring out who we are. For me, joy is a huge emotion, and it's very similar to how love feels. I believe joy runs on a spectrum, with some things bringing intense joy and some things providing a more 'lite' version.

It's taken me a long time to work out what gives me joy. Today, these things include looking at art, cooking, making art, writing and being with my partner and my friends. Just as it's important to incorporate our favourite places, people, scents, food and so on into our lives, joy is an essential ingredient in a happy life.

If you struggle with identifying emotions, it may be difficult to work out what joy even feels like. It may be easier to think about things that make you feel joyous on a physical level (if you feel emotions this way). Joy can raise our heart rate and make us feel physically warmer. Joy produces flow – the state of being deeply and happily engrossed in something. When we are in flow, we lose track of time and we can't wait to get back to doing the thing that brings us flow. Have you got something in your life that does this? Do more of that.

You are wonderful

The things that make you your wonderful and interesting self are all different threads woven together to create the tapestry of your life. I'm not being trite or patronizing when I say you are truly wonderful. You have so many interesting things about you. You have passions, interests, talents, skills, ideas and values. You also have needs and wants that are unique to you and that must be catered for.

When we come to know and understand ourselves, we are better equipped to form stronger relationships, both with ourselves and others. Through this process we build a solid foundation on which to build the rest of our lives.

Suzi's thoughts on getting to know yourself

How can I be my true unapologetic self? What if people don't like the real me? How do I unpeel the layers of protection I have, both consciously and unconsciously, built over the years?

Who even am I? How can I discover and present my true self?

A little at a time, at a pace and in a way that feels comfortable to you is the short answer.

You've probably spent your life being forced to do things in a way that has been painfully uncomfortable. Now it's time to give yourself permission to do things your way and at your own pace.

You get to choose how the rest of your life is lived, and essentially who you are and who you want to be.

For years, I thought my face was too fat to have very short hair. And, like Kate, I wore dark clothes to cover up my perceived larger body. In the last few years, I've had my hair cut very short (think of the awesome kickass popstar Pink). I have started wearing hot pink, purple and blue, which in true autistic style are my brand colours, too.

Also, in true autistic style I have now got a pair of pink, purple and blue trainers, which of course have to match to the pink, purple and blue jackets. And I always wear a cool print t-shirt to finish off the look. Also, I sometimes colour my hair pink (only when wearing my pink jacket, of course!)

Not even five years ago, I would never have been brave enough to express my true self through my short hair and bright clothes. I remember a hugely validating comment on a Facebook post. I said I'd never been brave enough in the past to have my hair like this and somebody commented, 'You look more like you now.' Wow! That was a special and defining moment for which I'm hugely grateful.

— Chapter 17 —

Finding the Confidence to Be Your True Self

SUZI

There are many advantages to building confidence and the good news is that anyone can become more confident if this is something they want. This chapter will explore confidence and offer ways to help you on your journey to having more confidence in your life.

What is confidence?

Feeling confident in ourselves can give us a solid foundation on which to build. When we are feeling confident, we are more likely to experience happiness, good relationships and an increase in self-esteem. We are more likely to try different things, advocate for ourselves (and others) and tap into our potential. Being confident allows us to speak our truth, unmask and not worry so much about what others think or say about us.

When we build confidence, we can have more trust in ourselves, set goals and live lives that are in alignment with our values. We can honour and respect our needs, communicate them to others and reinforce them when we need to (humans will always try to push each other's boundaries). See Chapter 5: Communication for how to confidently and assertively express needs and wants.

What gets in the way?

Fear. Fear of the unknown, of looking 'stupid', of failure and even of success. These are just a few factors. Throw into the mix the number of times many autistic folks get the messages that they are 'too much' or 'not enough' or if they 'could just do the thing', and it is not surprising that our confidence can be chipped away. We learn to play small and hide our true selves, including the wonderful things that make us uniquely us.

Nikki shared what helped her: 'Self-awareness, self-kindness, self-compassion, and just being able to change and adapt my life so that it supports me and doesn't work against me.'

Societal expectations can work against us autistic folks, which in turn can knock our confidence. That's why this chapter is about your confidence and not what 'society' says is correct, which, let's face it, is a load of BS anyway!

It is therefore important to realize that confidence means different things to different people and that is perfectly OK. It is also a personal choice as to when and how you build your confidence. A top tip: Do NOT compare yourself or your levels of confidence to that of others, as this is guaranteed to knock your confidence. Everyone's journey is unique, and although we share similarities, each of us is so different, with such wide and varied experiences, and our neurodivergence will also affect us differently.

Explore your confidence

Journal/write, make a mind map/video/voice note on the following questions:

- What does confidence mean to you?
- When do you feel most confident?
- When do you feel least confident?
- Think/write about a time when you felt confident. Where were you? What were you doing? How were you feeling?

On a scale of 0–10 (0 = not at all, 10 = absolutely) how confident do you feel about yourself right now?

What have you learned about yourself from answering the above questions?

Ways to build confidence

We need to have an idea of what we want and by setting a clear goal or intention we can start to work out what this is. Below are some examples which you can use or adapt. They are framed in positive language so that the brain knows exactly what is expected. They also start with 'I am' or 'I have' rather than 'I will be' so that the brain can get to work now and not at some moment in the future.

First, write down your goal/intention (see the examples below for ideas):

- I am confident.
- I am confident in myself and my abilities.
- I have healthy friendships and am confident in these.
- I have a happy/healthy relationship.
- I confidently express my needs and wants.
- I confidently advocate for myself.
- I am confident in myself when meeting new people.
- I am confident at work.
- I confidently say no to anything that does not serve me.
- I confidently stand up for myself.

Next, answer all or some of the following:

- What would achieving your chosen goal mean to you?
- How would your life be affected by achieving your goal?
- What would you like to be doing?
- What will you be saying? (What language will you be using?)
- What is motivating you to achieve your goal?

- How would you like to feel when achieving your goal?
- What would you like to be thinking?

Now, ask yourself 'reality questions':

- What is happening right now in relation to your chosen goal?
- What have you done already towards your goal?
- What is stopping you from doing more?
- What challenges are you facing regarding your goal?
- What are your barriers to success?
- What resources do you have available to help you (internet, YouTube, books, people)?
- Think of a similar goal that you have achieved in the past – what helped? What skills and strengths did you use?
- What do you believe about your ability to achieve this goal?

Next, have a look at 'options questions'. These questions are designed to get the creative part of your brain going and to prompt you to think of new possibilities. Try to write as many ideas as possible so that later you can choose a few that really appeal to you.

- What could you do to bring yourself closer to your goal?
- What is the easiest thing you could do straight away to help you move a step closer to your goal?
- What is something you could try that you haven't tried before?
- Who can help you with your goal?
- What is the fun option?
- What is the exciting option?
- What is the challenging option?
- How could you incorporate your passions and interests into working towards your goal?
- Looking at your barriers from the previous section, what could you do to overcome them?

- Looking at the challenges from the previous section, what could you do to overcome them?

Finally, ask yourself 'way forward questions'. This is where you make your mini plan to start your journey towards your goal/intention. Remember, you are in control and can change/adapt your plans at any point. (Top tip: choose two or three actions at a time – actions can be thoughts.)

- What option (from the previous section) will you try?
- What else?
- What option feels easy to achieve?
- What option feels exciting?
- What will you commit to trying?
- What do you think will help you achieve your goal?

It is hoped that by answering the questions you now have a clear goal and mini plan of action. It can help to share your goals with someone you trust, which can also help with accountability. It is also useful to review and adapt your goals as and when needed.

If you are serious about your goals and personal growth/development, then coaching can be of great benefit. When choosing a coach, it is wise to consider the following:

- Find three or four coaches whose websites/social media you are drawn to.
- Arrange a call with each of them to see who you click or get on with.
- Write down questions in advance of the calls about what their process is, what to expect from sessions, their costs and what their experience of autism is, plus any others you may have.

Final thoughts on confidence

I have not always been confident, and even when I acted/appeared confident, I never truly felt it. As I grew up, my confidence was chipped away at and the beliefs I formed kept me small and unconfident. Through a lot of personal development work (including comedy improvisation and coaching), grieving and healing, I now know what it is to be truly confident in myself and my abilities.

I hope I have given you some ideas on how to build your confidence, whatever that looks like to you. I believe that if we spend time pursuing our passions, interests and things we are good at, then the challenges we have are easier to tackle and overcome. By practising self-compassion, we can learn to be kind to ourselves and move forward on our journey of self-acceptance.

Please do more of what brings you joy, find ways to celebrate your unique skills and strengths, and learn to accept all parts of you, including your limitations. Seek support from people you trust. Even though this can be challenging, it is crucial to growth, to feeling connected and for belonging.

Finding other neurodivergent folks who get you, don't judge you and see you is life-changing, so I urge you to find those who understand you. We are not broken; we are perfectly imperfect (all humans are) and that is more than OK.

— Chapter 18 —

Thoughts, Beliefs and the Inner Critic

SUZI

How you think is a huge part of your journey of self-discovery and finding out who you really are. There is a lifetime of conditioning, masking and not knowing who you truly are to uncover. This, my friend, is not easy, but it is so worth it.

With awareness and understanding comes knowledge, freedom and personal power. You will start to unravel it all and become the person you were meant to be all along. You will become you. This is a vulnerable time where you are examining your whole self through a different lens. It is also a fantastically exciting time because the possibilities of who you are, what you can do and where you want to go are endless.

Many of the people interviewed for this book spoke of how liberating it is to find out that you are not broken, defective or a rubbish human. You are wonderfully, uniquely different and that is a good thing.

Our interviewees also talked about the importance of finding a tribe or community of other autistic adults with whom they can connect and share the ups and downs of life. Most importantly, we all seek a sense of true belonging.

For years, you may have felt as if you didn't belong, which could have led to feeling and being disconnected from others and yourself. Now is your time, my friend, to understand yourself, grieve and heal, and to transform. You are a wonderful human who has no doubt spent a lifetime feeling confused or sad and lost at times. The fact that you are reading this book right now shows that your time has come.

Please take from it what resonates and works for you and take your time. There is a lot to process, and over time you will no doubt need to process things and experiences more than once. Please understand that you are on a lifelong journey of self-discovery and the only person's pace that matters is yours.

This journey only really starts now that you have identified as being autistic. Be aware that others may be very different from you. This is because there is great diversity in autism and no two people will present the same. We all have our own unique personalities, experiences, upbringing and so on, and these will impact on your autistic presentation.

Comparing, although a natural human thing to do, is not always helpful, especially if it leads to thoughts such as 'I'm not like her; I'm not autistic enough' or 'I don't have it as bad as him'. These types of thoughts do not serve you or benefit you. They will only cause doubt and feelings of not being good enough, and I bet you have experienced a lifetime of those types of thoughts and feelings, haven't you?

Mindset is key. Our thoughts are what create our feelings. This is why there is such a high prevalence of mental health difficulties that sadly evolve with neurodivergent folk. In order to take control of our thoughts and to undo years of conditioning, we have to do the inner work to address our core beliefs and values, which is a powerful foundation on which to build.

By understanding what is important to us and why and what we truly believe about ourselves, we can start to question if we are living a life aligned to what we want and who we are. By examining our beliefs and our thoughts, we can choose to change them. We can literally rewire our brains to serve us and ultimately create our own happiness. I truly believe our purpose on earth is to be happy, and you and I both 100 per cent deserve to be happy. Powerful stuff.

Values

What are values? Put simply, they are the things that are important to us and that we care about. Our values, whether we are aware of them or not, act as a guide for us and determine how we act and what we do.

If we are in conflict with our values and not living in accordance with what feels good or right, we can feel out of sorts, unhappy and conflicted.

My top three values are fun, freedom and adventure, and if I am experiencing these three things in my life, then I feel aligned, happy and as if I have purpose. One of the many benefits of working for myself is living in alignment with my values.

Other values of mine (in no particular order) are:

- truth
- honesty
- creativity
- self-compassion
- helpfulness
- family
- love
- joy.

Many autistic folks have spent a long time in roles that are not aligned to their true selves or values. For example, I spent 17 years in a teaching career that, although aligned to my value of helpfulness, did not align to my core value of freedom. In fact, I felt trapped! I was trapped in a system that does not lend itself to the neurodivergent experience, where rules felt stifling and the curriculum rigid.

Why did I stay in education for so long? Good question! I think it was a mixture of getting used to the salary, which was pretty good, feeling as if I would be a failure if I stopped (pride and ego talking right there) and not realizing that just because I could do something, it didn't mean I should. I also thought that if I just carried on, then one day it would all be a lot easier than it was.

My role in my friendships was that of the clown, joker and risk taker, and while I had a lot of fun playing these roles, I did not always feel as if I was being true to myself or the true version of me. As you can see, truth is a value of mine, and to be misaligned in this way felt wrong, and there was a niggling discomfort that I couldn't quite identify.

Discovering what my values are and how much they influence my life was a complete game changer for me. I was able to think about what was honestly important to me and how I could add more of this to my life. It can take a long time to work out who you are and where you want to be, and I believe that values are like a guiding light, shining for us and helping us find our way in what can often be a dark and lonely place.

I'm sure you know that by covering up our true selves for so long, we can lose sight of who we are. That is why I am so passionate about values work and helping others realize what their own are so that they can make choices that feel good, aligned and purposeful.

IDENTIFY YOUR VALUES

What are your top ten values? Use the list below for starters and feel free to add any of your own.

- Honesty
- Respect
- Efficiency
- Trustworthiness
- Integrity
- Empathy
- Compassion
- Dependability

- Courage
- Loyalty
- Responsibility
- Equality
- Decisiveness
- Love
- Sustainability
- Creativity
- Joy
- Uniqueness
- Discretion
- Gratitude

How are your values being honoured in your relationships, career choices, personal development and overall sense of purpose? Are you happy with how your life and values are aligned? Is there room for improvement? What steps could you take to move closer to where you want to be? I wholeheartedly encourage you to write down what you want to achieve and a few small steps in the right direction that you are willing to take. It can be surprising just how quickly momentum and motivation can build.

Beliefs

A belief is a thought that we have repeatedly, and because of the automatic nature of the thought, we often accept it as the truth. Often it is not!

There is a lot of misinformation out there about autism, and stereotypes are still rife. How many times have you heard someone say, 'Oh, you don't look autistic'? What on earth? What absolute nonsense!

These types of comments are more damaging than the people saying them will ever know. Why? Because us literal autistic folk often believe what we hear, especially when we are first looking into the prospect of being autistic, which is scary and vulnerable in itself.

I've mentioned before that when I bravely found the courage to share that I thought I might be autistic with my manager at the time, whom I trusted and had so much respect for, I was devastated when she acted surprised and said, 'You are nothing like Roy from *Coronation Street*.' I was speechless and my heart felt wrenched. If you don't know about Roy and *Coronation Street*, he is a character in a British soap opera who I would say is stereotypically autistic. Let's just say, he is very different from me and all the other autistic women (and men and other genders actually) that I know. This interaction left me doubting myself and waiting five years before approaching the UK NHS for an autism assessment.

Many of the stereotypes leave us late-identified folk in a state of limbo, questioning and self-doubt. The media has us portrayed as either non-speaking savants like the character in the film *Rain Man* or as little boys who talk nonstop about trains or science; pretty much every piece of literature (and the diagnostic criteria) talks of difficulties with social skills. Well, I can relate to others, so how can I be autistic?

This is a far cry from the reality of our lives and experiences, and it is not surprising that we can pick up beliefs such as 'I can't be autistic, I have a great imagination', which I am sad to admit I said (before I knew better). Or 'I have lots of empathy, how can I possibly be autistic?' or another of mine, 'I'm bad at maths, I can't be autistic'. I now know that all these beliefs were and are untrue.

There is so much scope for developing beliefs that simply are not true when growing up with undiagnosed autism, and as we are so literal in our understanding of language, this is amplified. I did not even question what were facts and what were opinions until very late in life.

Unchecked beliefs that make us feel bad (our thoughts that create our feelings) can lead to low self-esteem, poor self-image and low self-worth. So many late-identified people I speak to talk about how they did not know themselves, what they liked or even what they wanted. This is why so many of us became chameleons in our behaviours, to blend in with who we were with at the time and what we perceived they wanted from us.

It saddens me to this day that I and many others unknowingly sacrificed our needs and wants in order to please others and to fit in. The good news is that once you know what you are dealing with, you can identify which beliefs are true and which are making you miserable. The beauty is that we can change them. We can literally rewire our brains with new thoughts that serve us, empower us and make life a heck of a lot better.

The inner critic

What if I can't change that voice in my head that tells me that I am 'no good at...(fill in the gap)' or that 'nobody likes me'? This voice is your inner critic, which is sometimes referred to as ego. The good news is that it is the part of your brain that is responsible for keeping you safe, and it certainly can be quietened to work in your favour if you know how.

Ego is the ancient part of your brain that has always been responsible for telling you to get to safety when you are actually in danger – for example, when you are running from a burning building or from a bear.

However, by doing its job, the ego can take things too far and step in to help when you are not in danger at all. Well, that is not entirely true. The danger that the ego is trying to protect you from is your emotions. If you are hurt by others' opinions of you, your ego quickly learns to step in and tell you things like 'Don't share your ideas with her, she will make fun of you', and before we know it, we are listening and responding to what our ego tells us, even if it tells you the same story about a completely different person that simply isn't true.

Now, it is still not a bad thing. How could it be? Its job is to protect you and keep you safe. That is an important job in my opinion. However, when we let the ego take control, we can stop being our true selves by hiding who we truly are. We can avoid people, places and situations, and live our lives in fear.

The first steps towards taking control and accepting the ego for what it is – a protector – is understanding what is happening and noticing when the ego is stepping in to 'help'. Then you can take back control and live your life how you want to.

Another way to soothe the ego is to talk to it. Either in your head or out loud, saying something like 'Thanks, ego, for trying to keep me safe but I am OK, I've got this'. I was amazed how different I started feeling when I began talking to my ego in this way. I immediately felt better, reassured and calmer.

Another factor affecting our belief systems is that of societal expectations. Examples of this are how eye contact supposedly shows a person's integrity or how a firm handshake makes you a strong candidate for a job. This is so ridiculous, but some people made this stuff up years ago and made it the rules. It is said that etiquette helps make everyone feel comfortable. Everyone? I don't think so! This type of conditioning gives the message that we should make others feel comfortable, even to the detriment of our own comfort. This, I believe, is how masking evolves and, as we know, the effects of doing so can be exhausting and often devastating.

How to change your beliefs

Here are some common beliefs neurodivergent folk pick up along the way and how they might impact on our lives. I've provided some new beliefs to help you change your thinking.

Belief	Possible outcome	New belief
I'm not good enough.	Not trying, staying the same, doing the same things, feelings of worthlessness and self-doubt.	I am enough.
I'm stupid.	Not trying, playing small, not speaking up, fear of looking stupid, fear of learning.	I learn differently and that is OK.
I'm a rubbish adult.	Comparing self to others who 'have it all together', worrying that people will judge unfairly, fear of being judged.	I find some things difficult and that is OK. I am developing at a pace that is right for me.
I am lazy.	Low self-esteem, confidence and self-worth. Unrealistic expectations of abilities. Feelings of embarrassment.	I am productive when interested and motivated.
I am flaky.	Thoughts of 'I can't be trusted' leading to low self-image. Pushing through and exceeding personal limits when you are likely overwhelmed and exhausted, possibly leading to burnout and poor physical and mental health.	I work with and honour my energy. It is OK to say no or to change my mind. I am honest about my capabilities.
I am disorganized.	Feelings of embarrassment and comparing self to others who appear to be organized. Avoidance of tasks that are difficult, possibly leading to missed appointments, missed payments and a sense of letting others down.	I am organized when I have the right tools and support to help me. I am learning organization skills (at my own pace).
I am flawed.	Low confidence and self-esteem. Hiding gifts and talents. Fear of judgement and ridicule.	I am perfectly imperfect and that is OK. I am awesome!

cont.

Belief	Possible outcome	New belief
I'm not as good as others at...(insert verb here) – comparisonitis!	Leads to heartache, self-judgement, unrealistic expectations.	I focus on myself. I can only control what I do. I am capable in lots of ways.
Nobody wants to hear what I have to say.	Feelings of self-doubt, avoidance of new people, fear of speaking up/giving opinions, avoidance of new/unfamiliar activities or situations. Possible isolation.	I need to feel safe with others.
I am socially awkward.	Fear of judgement/ridicule. Thoughts such as 'They will think I am weird'. Avoidance of situations. Fear of speaking in case you say the 'wrong' thing or unintentionally upset or offend. Loneliness/isolation.	I find some social situations difficult and that is OK. I feel safe in social situations when I feel accepted for who I am.
Nobody likes me.	Feelings of sadness, self-doubt, avoidance of others. Playing small, not being authentic, masking.	The right people like me. If people don't like me, that is OK, I am OK. I am likeable/lovable.
I am weird.	Comparing self to others who appear 'normal' and 'together'. Seeing self in a negative light, focusing on 'weirdness' rather than strengths and positive qualities.	I am different and that is OK. I am proud to be different.

Need I list more? I think this is more than enough, don't you? It saddens me that so many of us autistic folk grow to believe these thoughts as the truth. I am categorically telling you now that they are not the truth. They are messages you picked up along the way and your brain (ego part) told you they were true.

Now you know what has been happening, you can (if you choose) start to change any beliefs that you have that are not serving you. Look at the list of beliefs above and think about how each one would/does make you feel? I'm guessing that if you have these beliefs or similar ones, you feel quite awful each time you think about them.

Changing limiting beliefs

The key to changing beliefs is to start challenging them by asking yourself some questions. If you can journal/write/type your answers, you will hopefully start to see them in a different way. If this type of work is too triggering for you or you think, 'This is hopeless, it will never work for me', then maybe a therapist or counsellor might be the right option for you right now.

If you are keen to make the changes and happily answer the questions, maybe coaching could help you delve deeper into the beliefs that could be holding you back from achieving what you want in life.

Here are some questions to help you unlock any beliefs that are not serving you – for example, beliefs that make you feel less than, sad, angry, or are holding you back in some way.

First, make a list/table/spider diagram (or whatever works for you) of any of your limiting beliefs, then answer the following questions. Please note that you can answer some or all of them – choose whichever ones resonate with you.

- How is this belief serving you?
- What if the opposite were true?
- How would you feel if you no longer had this belief?
- What would change in your life if you no longer had this belief?

- What would be different about you if you no longer had this belief?
- What effect is this belief having on you?
- How could you reframe this belief?
- Is this belief true?
- What evidence do you have that this belief is true?
- What evidence do you have that this belief is false?
- What new belief would you like to have? What small steps could you take to start to create this new belief? What will you do to start to create this new belief?

Remember, just because you have carried these beliefs around with you for a lifetime, it does not mean they are true, and you certainly don't need to believe them anymore. In her interview, Morwenna said:

> It can take years to unlearn everything we've been told. Time and patience as well, I think, goes in there with acceptance. It doesn't happen overnight, and I think when you get a diagnosis, whether it's formal or self-realization, it takes years and years to unpick all of that, and you're still doing it years later, peeling the layers of the onion.

To challenge and change your beliefs takes time and effort – you are creating new neural pathways – so please take tiny steps, be patient and compassionate with yourself and, most of all, start to trust in the wonderful human that you are!

Morwenna said that when you notice the thoughts taking over, 'stopping and taking a few breaths and trying to catch the self-talk, that kind of inner critic' can help. She told me that she sometimes uses a set of questions in order to ground herself in reality, such as 'What would you say to your client, or what would you say to yourself, to your best friend?' and 'How would I feel if this was somebody else? I would feel compassion. I would feel like I would want to help them to not beat themselves up. It's empathizing for ourselves.'

Using your imagination for good

Add into the mix an imagination that can work both in our favour and against us. Our brains have become so evolved and advanced that, for many (not all), our imagination can be a great source of wonder, inspiration and enjoyment. It can also be a source of sadness, fear and resentment. How many times have you used your imagination to replay an embarrassing situation or conversation repeatedly? It's horrible, isn't it? One way to help is to recognize when your imagination is and is not serving you. When you are feeling good, try practising imagining good things happening, doing things you enjoy, what you are saying, how you are feeling, what others are saying to you. If we can intentionally use our imagination in this way, we can literally change our reality.

What are you spending time thinking about? Are you ruminating about all the times you said something 'wrong' or didn't catch on to the 'joke' that everyone else was laughing about? Or are you thinking about/replaying the times when things went well – for example, that time when you were there for a friend who was struggling? Are you thinking good things about yourself, such as 'My intentions are good', 'I am a kind and honest person', 'I am always doing my best with the tools I have got'?

Working with vision boards

If you find it difficult to imagine, then another way to think about good things that serve you is to create a simple vision board of things, which can also act as visual goals. There are many ways to create vision boards, such as electronically via apps. My personal favourite way is to cut or tear pictures and words from magazines and stick them on a plain piece of paper or card, neatly or haphazardly, whatever suits you.

If perfectionism is going to get in the way, it can be helpful to remind yourself that this is for your eyes only and the intention is to think about good things and certainly not to create the prettiest picture ever!

For me, the process is relaxing and absorbing. It allows my brain to slow down and reflect on the things that are important to me, what good I am doing in the world and what I truly want in my future.

Ideas for vision board focus

- All about me: All the *good* things, likes, strengths, skills, qualities, achievements and so on.
- My future: What you would like your future to be like, what you would like to be doing, where you would like to live. What you will you have. Who you will be with.

Vision boards can be a fun and creative way to think about the future and how you would like it to be. They can also serve as a reminder to those of us whose memories are, let's say, 'challenged'. Visual prompts can be so helpful for us neurodivergent folks in reminding us of our hopes and dreams as well as helping us maintain focus on what we want.

However you choose to explore your beliefs and identify when that pesky inner critic is talking the loudest is, of course, entirely up to you. I hope this chapter has got you thinking about how adaptable the brain is and how new neural pathways can be made.

Remember, your brain will resist change. That's the ego's job: to keep things the same as it believes that same equals safety. In times of resistance and change, try gently reassuring your ego that all is well and these changes are for the better, and of course you are perfectly safe.

— Chapter 19 —

Focus on Your Strengths and Create the Life You Want

SUZI

The more you know and celebrate and live your super gifts and your passions...it's a really wonderful life.

SARAH

Many autistic folks have received messages that they are not enough, are too much and are lacking in all sorts of ways. The diagnostic criteria have had a hand in this narrative as they focus on deficits. Even the 'official' name suggests that there is something wrong and includes the word 'disorder'. Alice illustrated this point eloquently when she said, 'We only recognize autism in people when we see the outward signs of distress, and the outward distress is [one of] the diagnostic criteria for an autism assessment as well.'

The narrative is changing but there is still a long way to go. There is nothing to stop us fabulous autistic folk focusing on our strengths and creating the lives we want to live. I would go as far as to say that it is imperative that we identify, build on and focus on our individual strengths if we are to be truly, authentically and unapologetically happy with who we are.

Every autistic person is different. However, there are many strengths that are associated with autism, such as being honest, empathic, determined, focused, justice driven, passionate, creative and able to recognize patterns, to name a few.

If you are not used to thinking about what is great about you, then it may feel a bit strange at first, but remember, anything different involves change, and change can take us autistic folks longer to process. The key is to start small and build from there.

So how do we focus on our strengths when our neural pathways have been moulded to focus on our challenges? We decide to do it. That's it. We get to choose where we spend our energy and what we focus on. The brain is wonderful in so many ways, and the good news is that it can be changed and remoulded in ways that serve us and help us to feel confident and to be happy!

This of take time, work and effort, of course, but that's something we can tap into, right? We autistic folks have great abilities when it comes to learning about our passions and interests. The key is to take these skills and apply them to focusing on our strengths. We must do more of the things we are good at/feel passionate about and take time to recognize our strengths and to utilize them in a mindful way.

Strengths-finder activity

Make a list of your strengths and skills (use Google to provide you with a list to get you started or ask someone you trust to help you). Strengths quizzes and questionnaires can be found online, which can also be a useful starting point.

Journal/write/create a spreadsheet and give a real-life example of when you demonstrated/used that strength or skill (no matter how small or insignificant you feel it is).

Spend time thinking about how good you are at...(insert strength here) and notice how you are feeling. Our thoughts directly influence our feelings, so it is to be hoped that you are having positive feelings when thinking about your strengths.

The more time spent thinking about your strengths, skills and what you enjoy doing, the more positive feelings you will experience, and these in turn will influence your behaviour (your actions/what you do). For example, one of my strengths is performing and this is something I love to do.

While consciously thinking about performing and how I felt when I had a lead role in a comedy murder mystery play, I realized that I wanted to do more of this, so I set about looking for some local auditions and ended up fulfilling a dream I had had for a while, which was to appear in a musical theatre production. This was amazing (and hard work). Had I not reflected on my love of performing and how I felt before, I would not have taken action (fuelled by my thoughts and feelings) and found a local musical theatre production.

Thinking about our strengths in this way can be applied to all areas of life and can help build self-esteem and confidence. I know this, because it is what I and many of my clients have done. Is this something you want and will commit to? Who can help you? What will life be like if things stay the same? What is stopping you doing some strengths work? How can you overcome this? What is one thing you will do today to start your strengths discovery journey?

Turn your passion into a job

Many autistic people spend a long time in jobs and careers that are not suited to them. This can contribute to challenges with mental health and wellbeing, and to stress, anxiety and burnout. Michelle had many jobs before setting up her own business and said, 'Essentially the anxiety, depression and sense of not belonging was present in every job, and I struggled to fit in often.'

It's not surprising that so many autistic folks carve careers and businesses out of their passions and interests. It can be soul-destroying doing a job that gives no pleasure, purpose or enjoyment. It is so much harder for the autistic population to make themselves do something for the sake of it. In my experience of being autistic and working with hundreds of autistic children, young people and adults, I have noticed that if interest is piqued, then it is much easier to do the thing, whatever that may be.

Michelle, an autistic ADHDer and ex-primary school teacher, has combined her passions for writing and people. 'My fascination is people, stories and the way people make meaning in the world. I am fascinated by our brains.' She now runs a community interest company with her husband, supporting writers and theatre makers to network and attend writing retreats. She is also a business coach. Like many other neurodivergent folks, she has had a lot of different jobs in the past and has now found what works for her.

One area of interest and passion for me throughout my lifetime has been people. Being autistic and not knowing it for 36 years (I'm now 48), I was always fascinated (and often confused) by people and their behaviour. From secondary school onwards, I learned that people were not always what they seemed. Suddenly, there were (unwritten) rules about who was 'cool' and who was not, and people would rarely say what they meant.

I unconsciously made it my life's work to understand human behaviour and, as a teen, devoured the problem pages in magazines like *Just Seventeen*. I later became a teacher and specialized in working with students with social, emotional and mental health challenges.

I put my passion for studying humans (it's not over yet, as I now coach them) down to being autistic. I am grateful that I am autistic, as I'm pretty sure I would not otherwise have studied them to the depth that I have.

For 17 years I worked as a teacher in various mainstream and alternative education settings. Being a teacher was hard. Being undiagnosed autistic, ADHD, Tourette's and OCD made it even harder. There were elements of teaching that I loved, such as teaching the students. I was passionate about delivering fun and interesting lessons and at my best I was an 'outstanding teacher'. However, the difficulties far outweighed the good bits. The constant planning, assessing, recording and reporting, the politics, noise, crowds and endless meetings were hard. Also, I didn't know what my needs were, so I was not honouring or communicating them.

It was tough! I now know that the challenges were related to executive functioning, sensory differences and social expectations – a neurodivergent's nightmare! After many burnouts, bouts of depression and anxiety, I eventually saw the light and quit!

Throughout my healing journey, I have asked myself why I stayed in teaching for so long, and the sad truth is that I thought I 'should' be able to handle it, that it would get easier if I tried harder, and I felt that my identity was tied up in being a 'teacher'. I now know that just because I can do something does not mean that I should. We have so many transferable skills, qualities and strengths that we can apply to areas that nourish us and align with our values once we know where to look.

In 2020, the world changed due to Covid, and I was in a fortunate position to be able to start my own business based on my interests, passions and energy. By working one to one as a coach, I can align my values of helping others in a way that does not drain my energy. My passion for stand-up and improvised comedy, which has helped me transform as a person, is part of my business, as is speaking at events and conferences to help audiences understand what autism and ADHD are and how to support neurodivergent colleagues, clients and loved ones. I am living my passions and interests day in, day out, and can honestly say I have never felt happier or more fulfilled!

Whether you would like to start your own business or are looking for a job with someone else, it is well worth trying to find an area that aligns with your values and interests.

It is worth mentioning that I and many others have been able to pursue our passions through work by utilizing support from others. In England, Scotland and Wales there is government funding available for business/work support through a scheme called Access to Work (eligibility criteria apply), and Northern Ireland has its own scheme, Access to Work (NI). If you are outside the UK, please check for local services that may be available for you, too.

So, in an ideal world, what would you do for work? If nothing was stopping you, what would you love to do?

If the above questions feel too big, how about making a list or spider diagram of your passions and interests and researching jobs, careers and businesses related to them?

It can be helpful to connect with others who have already made their passions work for them. Support groups and social media groups for neurodivergent business owners are plentiful in the online space. There are many coaches who can support you to find clarity on what you want and how to take the first steps. If you have friends, family and people you can trust, then sharing ideas with them can help you get clear and get started.

Remember, strengths + passions = one happy autistic person!

How to begin crafting your best life

If you want to align your values, needs and interests with a job/career/business that works for you, where do you start? I hope this book and the activities within it will have helped you work out what your needs are, where your strengths lie and what your values are.

The following questions will help you explore what is possible and lead you to your first steps on the path to a job, career or business that works for you.

Write, type or journal the answers to all/some of the following:

- In an ideal world, what would you like to spend most of your time doing?
- What would your ideal day be like? Consider everything that you would like it to include – for example, breakfast, exercise, fun stuff, time in nature, work, TV/reading and so on.
- If you could wave a magic wand, what job/business would you choose?

- If there was nothing stopping you, what would you do?
- What is stopping you doing what you want to do? Make a list.
- What could you do to overcome these barriers?
- What resources are available to you? Friends, family, social media business groups, online quizzes, coaches, charities, organizations and so on?
- What could you do to explore your options further?
- What strengths and skills can you tap into to help with this?
- What could you do to move one step toward your ideal job/career/business?
- What else could you do?
- Looking at all your answers, what can you do today that will move you forward?
- What will you do?

These questions can be explored in several ways, and if you can discuss them with someone, it may help you gain clarity in what you want and how to go about achieving it. I suggest taking time to work on them. For example, aim to work on two questions per day over a week. Get creative and make it work for you, because, as we know, no two people are the same and there cannot be a one-size-fits-all approach; it simply does not work.

Good luck with creating a life that is aligned to you, your preferences, your needs, and your values. It is possible to live a happy and fulfilling life. It takes trial, error and experimentation but is so worth it!

Kate's thoughts on creating the life you want

I now live what I call a 'handpicked life'. It is very rare that I do anything I don't want to do. It has taken me a long time to get to this place. It's taken a lot of soul searching and trial and error.

Due to my daughter's very complex needs, my main income is state benefits. However, I still work because this gives me huge pleasure and satisfaction. My core work is around supporting parents and carers of autistic children. My specific niche is supporting parents who are just starting out on their autism journey. Before I recognized that this was my specialist area, I was trying to be all things to all parents, which wasted a lot of time and energy.

Part of the research for this book involved talking to interviewees about their sensory differences. During this process I thought, 'I don't really have many sensory differences.' It then occurred to me that I do actually have a lot of sensory differences, but I've carved out a life that factors these in.

I work from home, and my flat is organized around my and my daughter's sensory needs. We are both visual sensory seekers, so our home is full of fairy lights, glitter lamps and sparkly things. I use fragrance-free washing powder. I rarely turn on overhead lights; I have a lot of lamps and colour-changing LED lights instead. We almost always have calming music playing in every room.

All of my friends are neurodivergent. We meet at times and in places that suit our needs. I need a lot of sensory stimuli so seek out ways to ensure that these needs are met. I also ensure that I have deep down time when I can rest and recharge.

My work is constantly evolving. My daughter is permanently out of school and essentially home educated. This presents some challenges in terms of the time available to work. I've learned how to work around it. As I type, she is asleep, and I know I have at least another hour to work and that I'll be able to do more writing later.

I run training sessions and parent consultations via Zoom. I mainly do this when my daughter is with her dad, but it's not impossible to do when she is here. This is my second book and I'm already planning the third. Writing is something I can do anywhere, and I often write via the notes app on my phone.

Whatever your circumstances, positive change is possible. Whatever challenges you face can be worked around. As Suzi mentions, we can all come to understand our energetic needs and work around these. I am a morning person. You might be a night person.

FOCUS ON YOUR STRENGTHS AND CREATE THE LIFE YOU WANT

As we finish writing this book, it is the end of July. I won't work again until September. I know from experience that my brain turns to mush at this time of year, so there's no point in scheduling anything in or giving myself work that has any sort of deadline.

When I split up with my ex-partner, I took around three months off. I postponed everything that had been scheduled. After I'd had a good rest, normal service resumed. It would have been pointless (and very stressful) to try to work during that time.

My point is that you, too, can work around whatever is going on in your life. You may have some huge decisions to make. I had to do this when it became clear that my daughter was not going to be in school. As I've mentioned elsewhere, I also ended relationships with my ex-partner and with other people in my life. These were huge choices, but they've all brought me peace and contentment.

The beauty of getting older is that we can use our life experiences to gain a better understanding of ourselves. We can take stock of all of the work situations, relationships and friendships we've had and pick and choose what we want moving forward. It won't happen overnight, but when you take one step at a time, you will eventually reach your destination. It's well worth it, however many steps and years it takes.

— Chapter 20 —

Where Do We Go from Here?

KATE

After some time in your new, autism-centric life, you may notice that there are people who have very definite ideas on how to be autistic. There are specific words to use and specific ways to talk about autism.

I want you to understand that however you want to refer to yourself and however you choose to be in the world as an autistic adult is your choice. Whatever you choose is right for you and doesn't make you a less good autistic person.

Language

Over the 12 years I have worked in the autism field, the language around autism has changed greatly, and the pace seems to be quickening now. I am an autism specialist and even I have difficulty keeping up with the 'correct' language. At times, this has led me to feel that I am a bad autistic person, which is not a great feeling.

The language used around autism is hotly debated. The general consensus is that autistic adults prefer what is called 'identity first' language, saying about themselves, 'I am autistic' (an autistic person). This is opposed to 'person first' language, which would be 'I have autism' (a person with autism).

Similarly, there is also a lot of discussion around the use of the terms 'autism spectrum disorder (ASD)' and 'autism spectrum condition (ASC)'. Some feel it's inappropriate to call it a 'disorder', as we are not disordered individuals. Some feel it's inappropriate to refer to it as a 'condition' as it's simply part of our makeup.

However, some people say 'I am autistic' and some people choose 'I have autism'. Some people say 'I have ASD' or even 'I am ASD'. Or they may choose to say the same but use 'ASC' instead.

I found it interesting that in the chapter on PDA, Suzi says, 'I am PDA.' Some people who are both autistic and have ADHD refer to themselves as 'AuDHD'. (Interestingly, there is no person- or identity-first language debate regarding ADHD; it seems a very autism-specific issue.)

The bottom line is that it is your choice how you want to refer to yourself. Whatever you are comfortable with is right for you. It's possible that you may choose one way to refer to yourself now, but this may change in the future.

Quiet v loud

There are some amazing autistic autism advocates who are prolific content creators. These are people who question and push back on society's view of autism and treatment of autistic individuals. There are also people like me, who write and talk about autism and teach other people about it. There are also millions of autistic people, quietly going about their lives, not saying a word about autism or their autistic experience.

Just as with the language you choose, the way you present as autistic in the world is up to you. Some people feel compelled to talk about it and raise awareness. This is valuable and important. However, if this is not for you, that is perfectly fine.

I have found it useful to remind myself that the people who have the energy and time to be prolific creators and advocates likely have very different lives to me. I am a single parent with a child who is permanently out of school. While I would love to travel and speak and write and create a great deal more social media content than I do, this is impossible for me. Equally, if being a public face for autism advocacy just simply isn't your thing, then you don't have to do that.

Slowly, slowly

At the beginning of this book, I advised you to take 'quiet baby steps' as you make your way in what is a new world for you. I remind you of this again, here. Please take your time in working out what you need for yourself.

There's no timeline or deadline for you to settle into what being autistic will look and feel like for you. As we've shared in the previous chapters, there's a lot to get your head around. You've got a great deal of information to assimilate and find places for in your mind.

You are wonderful. You are interesting. You are creative and clever.

We see you and we wish you all the very best on your journey.

With huge love, care and affection,
Kate and Suzi x

Endnotes

Foreword
1. Newscientist.com. (2016). Letter: Editor's pick: Autism, empathy and compassion. *New Scientist* [online]. Accessed on 15 August 2024 at www.newscientist.com/letter/mg23030751-400-1-editors-pick-autism-empathy-and-compassion

Introduction
1. *Emergent Divergence: The neurodivergent ramblings of David Gray-Hammond* (December 2023) We need to talk about what it's like to discover you're neurodivergent. Facebook: www.facebook.com/reel/265715806012327

Chapter 2
1. The Equality Act 2010, Section 6: Disability. Available at www.legislation.gov.uk/ukpga/2010/15/section/6
2. HM Government (2024) Financial Help if You're Disabled. Available at www.gov.uk/financial-help-disabled

Chapter 3
1. Bellis, T.J. (2017) *When the Brain Can't Hear: Unravelling the Mystery of Auditory Processing Disorder*. New York, NY: Atria Books.
2. On The Spectrum Foundation (2023) Twice Exceptional. Accessed on 30 July 2024 at www.onthespectrumfoundation.org/twice-exceptional
3. Penzol, M. et al. (2019) *Functional Gastrointestinal Disease in Autism Spectrum Disorder: A Retrospective Descriptive Study in a Clinical Sample*. Bethesda, MD: National Library of Medicine.

4   Engelbrecht, N. (2023) *Autism and Eating Disorders*. Toronto: Embrace Autism. Accessed on 30 July 2024 at https://embrace-autism.com/autism-and-eating-disorders

Chapter 5

1   Laine-Toner, K. (2023) *Where Do I Start? How to Navigate the Emotional Journey of Autism Parenting*. London: Jessica Kingsley Publishers, p.61.

Chapter 7

1   Hu. C. (2024) Why writing by hand is better for memory. *Scientific American*. Accessed 17 July 2024 at www.scientificamerican.com/article/why-writing-by-hand-is-better-for-memory-and-learning
2   Brady, F. (2023) *Strong Female Character*. London: Jessica Kingsley Publishers.

Chapter 8

1   David Gray-Hammond (2023) December. Available at www.facebook.com/reel/894112625394468

Chapter 10

1   Autism & PDA (2024) PDA Society. Accessed on June 2024 at www.pdasociety.org.uk/what-is-pda-menu/about-autism-and-pda
2   Brown, B. (2021) *Atlas of the Heart: Mapping Meaningful Connection and the Language of Human Experience*. London: Vermilion.

Chapter 12

1   McLeod S. (2024) Maslow's Hierarchy of Needs. Simply Psychology. Accessed on 19 January 2025 at www.simplypsychology.org/maslow.html

Chapter 14

1   Mendes, E.A. (2023) *Armchair Conversations on Love and Autism: Secrets of Happy Neurodiverse Couples*. London: Jessica Kingsley Publishers.
2   Dattaro, L. (2020) Largest study to date confirms overlap between autism and gender diversity. Accessed on 23 July 2024 at www.thetransmitter.org/spectrum/largest-study-to-date-confirms-overlap-between-autism-and-gender-diversity/?fspec=1
3   List of gender identities. (2024) Wikipedia. Accessed on 23 July 2024 at https://en.wikipedia.org/wiki/List_of_gender_identities
4   Weir, E., Allison, C. & Baron-Cohen, S. (2021) *The Sexual Health, Orientation, and Activity of Autistic Adolescents and Adults*. Wiley. Accessed on 23 July 2024 at https://onlinelibrary.wiley.com/doi/10.1002/aur.2604

5   Mendes, Eva A. & Maroney, M. (2019) *Gender Identity, Sexuality and Autism.* London: Jessica Kingsley Publishers.
6   Pearson, A. & Hodgetts, S. (2023) 'Comforting, Reassuring, and...Hot': A qualitative exploration of engaging in bondage, discipline, domination, submission, sadism, (sado)masochism and kink from the perspective of autistic adults. *Autism in Adulthood.* Accessed on 24 July 2024 at www.liebertpub.com/doi/10.1089/aut.2022.0103
7   Powell, A. (2023) How social isolation, loneliness can shorten life. *The Harvard Gazette.* Accessed on 24 July 2024 at https://news.harvard.edu/gazette/story/2023/10/how-social-isolation-loneliness-can-shorten-your-life

Chapter 15

1   Murray, M. (2022) Monotropism: An Interest-Based Account of Autism. Accessed on 19 January 2025 at https://monotropism.org/dinah/monotropism-2020
2   Ruiz, D.M. (2008) *The Four Agreements: Practical Guide to Personal Freedom: A Practical Guide to Personal Freedom* (A Toltec Wisdom Book). San Rafael, CA: Amber-Allen Publishing.
3   Mohr, T. (2015) *Playing Big: For Women Who Want to Speak Up, Stand Out and Lead.* London: Arrow Books.